Footprints Of My Life

By
Patricia Ann Blake

Published in the United Kingdom.
Published by Mrs Patricia Ann Blake.
Printed in the United Kingdom by Baskerville Press.
Content and photographs © Patricia Blake 2013.

First printed 2013

ISBN 978-0-9926325-0-2

Introduction

How I came to write this book.

As my mother's carer, I used to take her to her hospital appointments in her wheel chair. Her Rheumatologist asked me what I felt about my mother being in all this pain, I said "I do sympathise because I suffer in the same way. Well, I take painkillers and anti-inflammatory drugs." "But you haven't seen me yet", he replied. "Well, ask your doctor to refer you, I will be happy to see you". I became one of his patients, and at one of my appointments he asked about my mother and said, "you have a lovely mother". I replied, "You don't know what you are talking about", and burst into tears.
He asked me to tell him about it, and then said write about it, it will heal your soul.

It took me five years to think about it, as I thought it would be disloyal.

In the end I thought, why not?

To Maria

Best Wishes

Trish

1

My earliest memories are of a children's home, I am not sure why, I my brother and sister were there, but it was something that was to be repeated, all through our childhood.

Whenever our parents fell out with each other, whether it was financial reasons or, some other reason, we children were shipped off somewhere; and when they made it up again we were brought back home again.

The first time we were sent away, I was two years old; my younger sister was still a baby in arms; we never found out what happened to our brother. It's too late to ask him now; as he died on the second of December 2000 at the age of sixty six.

We lived an extremely difficult life. I think most people would have cracked under the strain. Thank God we were made of stronger stuff. It probably comes from mixed breeding; we are what I call a Heinz fifty seven variety. On my father's side it's Scottish and English and on my mother's side it's Irish, Portuguese and German. No matter where in the world your ancestors came from if you lived in India for two or three generations, you were classed as Anglo Indian so that is what we are.

My brother Denzil, my sister Janet, and I were born in Kolar Gold Fields, Southern India in the K.G.F. Hospital and baptised in a church called St Michael and All Angels.

My father was James Jardine Murray who at the time worked as a timekeeper in the gold mines. My mother was Mildred Iris Ann (known as Iris) her maiden name was Muller. After we left Kolar Goldfields to live in Bangalore we rented a place in Palm Grove road. We did not stay there long as it was too expensive. We then moved, to Austin Town, where the bungalows were smaller and cheaper. There were two sizes, the big ones were ten rupees a month and the small ones were five rupees a month; Nana already lived in a five rupee one so we rented a ten rupee one and nana moved in with us to save paying two lots of rent.

I was rather a sickly child, so I did not start school till I was five and a half at the Good Shepherd convent; we were not catholic but it was considered the best education and as schools were not free, we had to get our money's worth. Shortly after that my sister Janet joined me at school, she was very cute and the nuns made a great fuss over her, the only attention I ever got was punishment which made me hate her all the more. My mother always played us off against each other which did not help our relationship.

Mum used to cut my hair, very short, to my earlobes; she said it was for my own good, she said my hair took all my strength away and to add insult to injury, it was my job to take my sister to a lady down the road to have her hair done in ringlets like Shirley Temple; when I asked why I could not have my hair done the same as my sister, mum said yours is too straight to bother with. Nana was very strict with us and would punish us when she thought it was necessary; mother on the other hand would lash out for the slightest reason. It was not unusual for mum to hit nana if she disagreed with her; anyway one day mum came home to find me crying, she asked why and I said "nana hit me", "hit her back" she said, so I did and nana told me "just for that the devil will come to see you tonight," whether it was my imagination or whether it was real I will never know but that night I saw him in all his glory, this black thing with horns, red eyes and tail, I ran to my nanas bed and begged, her forgiveness," I told you so" she said and she let me stay with her the rest of the night.

My brother Denzil was the kindest, most gentle human being I have ever known. He was very protective of his sisters; even if he got hurt in the process; He would give you the shirt off his back if you needed it. I'm afraid I used to bully him and he took it all without complaint.

My brother and I were great pals and we sometimes played at being Tarzan and Jane; I was also the only girl in a gang of boys, playing all the boys games, like football, flying kites, even boxing. We used to climb trees, even climb on to the roof of our bungalow. My sister always wanted to do the same but we said she couldn't because if she got hurt we would be in trouble; she then said, if we did not take her with us she would tell mum; she would run indoors, shouting "mummy mummy, Patsy and Denzil are on the roof or "mummy mummy, Patsy and Denzil are climbing trees;" then mum would come to find us with a stick in her hand, order us down and give us both a good hiding.

I have only seen my brother angry with me twice; once when I was wreaking revenge on my sister Janet and once when I almost made us late, going home from school, he knew we would be in trouble. The reason for the delay was, a wild flower we called, touch me not, it was a low growing plant with compound leaves and a fluffy pink flower, if you touched it, the leaves would close; so I went along touching all these leaves, which made us late; so in his frustration he hit me on the head with a coffee bottle.

I was a wilful stubborn child, insanely jealous of my two younger siblings. Not without reason. My mother never seemed to have time for me at all and I was very resentful. I remember my mother used to croon to Janet, " whose baby are you," my sister used to sing back "mummies baby are me" I used to seethe with jealousy because I never got that kind of attention; if I tried to emulate my sister, mother would say, grow up, your not a baby. I don't ever remember ever getting a kiss or a cuddle from her; even in adulthood, if you went to give her a kiss, she would turn her face away and offer you her cheek.

Janet was a mummy's baby and she knew how to work it. We spent our childhood and early teens in a love hate relationship; she could do no wrong until the youngest sister was born, after that she was no longer the blue eyed girl. Strangely enough, as much as I hated her and would get my revenge, whenever possible, I would never let any one else hurt her.

She was always getting into trouble with the big girls, by telling tales on them and then come to me for protection.

The youngest girl, Geraldine was always a spoilt brat, the less said about her the better. Mother frequently told me, that I was almost born in the toilet and that is where she should have left me; that made me feel worthless; I thought it was maybe, because I looked like my father.

When the Second World War began my father joined the Royal Navy. He became a chief petty officer, we never saw much of him after that; just the usual shore leave; we looked forward to his leave, with fear and dread, we knew what to expect; my father was a sadist, he enjoyed putting us all, including my mother through mental and physical torture.

For instance, he would show my mother photographs, of all the women he had been with, and compare them to her; he said he had a wife in every port. Sometimes he tied her hand and foot, like an oven ready chicken, put a knife to her throat and ask us children if he could push it in, he would then ask us who we loved the best, him or her. If he did not get the desired answer, we'd be beaten. I think he could put the Marquis De Sade to shame. He never lost his temper; everything he did was cold and calculated; I was two years old when I remember my first beating. I was caught playing with water in the bathroom; apparently, I was ladling water with my potty, from the big water container. He stripped me of all my clothes, folded them in a neat pile, removed his belt and beat me till my body was pulp. That's how it always was; He took his time and he enjoyed our anticipation.

Whenever he got shore leave, we used to have to pack up, and go to Bombay for the duration of his leave. It used to take three days and two nights, to go from Bangalore to Bombay by train.

We stayed in a fifth floor apartment in Collaba, not far from the Gateway of India. We had some fun times, when we stayed in Bombay.

The family next door were very friendly and their young son, who we used to call Ginger, was a special friend of mine. I was a tomboy and he was a bit of a tearaway and we were always getting into trouble, like sliding down the banisters from five floors up. Once I fell through the banisters, from the first floor to the ground floor and broke my arm, the people downstairs poured a bucket of water over me to revive me and sent for mother, she saw my wet body and thought I had drowned. I spent the rest of the holiday in plaster, I then had to have the plaster cut off and reset, because red ants crawled inside the plaster and stung me badly. I must have been a nightmare.

At that age I used to walk and talk in my sleep. On one occasion my mother came into the bedroom to find me sitting on the window ledge, waving goodbye to my father, it was five floors up and a sheer drop to the street, she picked me up and put me back in my bed, without waking me. On another occasion, apparently I got out of bed went through the front door, went next door used their toilet turned round and went back to bed. Nobody woke me they just told me about it in the morning.

On one of our visits to Bombay, we went to a holiday resort called Juhu, it was right on the beach, it consisted of disused busses, single and double decker, converted into holiday lets; I don't think father was with us that time, perhaps he had gone back to sea; we went with our neighbours, it was the happiest I can remember. We had been there about a week or so when a newspaper company, The Times of India came to spend time there. I don't know if they were on holiday or if they were celebrating something, but it turned into a tragedy; some of the men went swimming and went too far out and three men got swept away and drowned. There were flying boats searching for them but could not save them. It took three days for their bloated bodies to be washed ashore and after the fish had got to them, they were not a pretty sight. We children saw the bodies, it was not pleasant and mother decided we had to leave.

I remember our last Christmas holiday in Collaba we were all invited to a party in one of the apartments on the ground floor. It was a big affair and my father arrived dressed in my mothers black cocktail dress and made up to look like a woman. Some people were amused others were not; it wasn't seemly in those days; I think it was the last holiday we had in Collaba.

When I was about six and a half years old mum decided to get her own back on dad and got herself a boyfriend. His name was Mr. Jackson. He was a sergeant in the British army. Nana would have nothing to do with it so mum moved to a new address in Castle Street in Cox Town and although he never lived with us he certainly spent a lot of time there.

On my seventh birthday, we were taken to the local milk bar as a treat and we were given an ice cream sundae each; my sister Janet, disgraced herself by picking up the glass and draining it to the last drop, my brother and myself, kicked her under the table to make her behave, hoping she would realise it was not ladylike but all she said in a loud voice was, "WHAT".

Shortly after my birthday, someone wrote to my father and told him about mum's affair; he took compassionate leave from the navy and travelled back to Bangalore without telling anyone and arrived while we children were at school. He tied her hand and foot, used a cosh on her head, broke her nose, branded her face with a piece of wood from the fire and told her he was going to make sure that no man would look at her again; her screams brought the neighbours in and they called the police, they locked him up for three days and then let him out, someone had stood bail.

When we got home from school it was total confusion, no one would tell us what happened, the neighbours took us in until dad was released from jail; he then took us two girls by train to Mysore to a convent called St Philomina's and left us there with instructions never to let my mother know where we were; my brother was put in a boarding school who were given the same instructions.

Mother had been taken to hospital and it took a long time to heal her wounds, he also cut all her hair off; when she recovered, she found she had no family and try as she might, no one would tell her where we were.

My father was cashiered from the navy for what he had done but he was able to join the army, the R.E's.

While we were in the convent in Bangalore we were day scholars so we had no experience as boarders, so it came as a great shock when we went to Mysore, we did not realise strangers could be so cruel and unkind, especially nuns and priests, we expected, holy people to be kind at least. They reduced me to a nervous wreck I even developed a facial tic. They tried to brain wash us into becoming Roman Catholic and were punished if we did not comply. We had to do penance for every little thing we did wrong; one of the penances was to kneel on gravel for twenty minutes at a time. If we did not know our catechism by heart, we would get the ruler across the knuckles, sharp end on and if anyone wet the bed, during the night young and as little as we were we were made to carry our own mattress out into the sun to dry.

You could say, I was more like an oak than a willow, I would not bend my will for anyone and usually came off worst; I had a running battle with the nuns, we had to go to church every morning before going to school, we were made to wear veils, I would pull mine off so they resorted to putting elastic through mine, I still managed to pull mine off; we also had to carry a rosary, I had no idea what they were for so I used to play with mine and was usually punished.

One day we had a visit from a bishop, or someone who wore red, anyway we were all expected to line up and kiss his ring; needless to say I would not, all the others got a gift for doing this, I of course was punished and told I was a child of Satan. Once I was summoned to the mother superiors office; she told me if she ever saw me twitch my face again, she would chop my head off, she showed me a long thin bladed knife and said that was what she was going to use.

There was an older girl, I don't remember her Christian name but her surname was McGregor, she was a boarder; she had no mother and obviously her father had to work. She was a pretty and popular girl. One day the nuns received news that her father had died, that meant there would be no more school fees as she was now an orphan; without more ado and before the girl had time to mourn, she was stripped of her posh school uniform and given an orphanage dress to wear and marched off to the orphanage. We were not allowed to talk to her after that, I hate to think what her life was like after that.

There was an interesting and exciting side to life in the convent. From our dormitory, we could see the Maharaja's palace, it stood on a hill opposite. On the side of the hill facing the convent, was an enormous crocodile in electric lights, quite impressive; on one occasion, the school was invited to see the procession for the maharaja's birthday. Every year, he was supposedly weighed in gold; we did not witness this but we were invited to look round his stables; all the horses, elephants and camels decked out in reds, greens and gold it was quite a sight to behold.

After being at the convent for about a year, my father stopped paying the fees; obviously on army pay, he could no longer afford to; the nuns were not about to keep us for nothing, so they wrote to mum to come and remove us, which she did, thank goodness. Now I don't know where the money came from to keep my mother in hospital or what we lived on when we went back home; unless it was an allowance from the army, but we moved back to Austin town into one of the ten Rupee bungalow's, and nana moved back in with us.

2

We started school at Baldwin's High School for girls and my brother went to Baldwin's High School for boys; the two schools were about a mile apart, I was eight and my sister was six and a half. Up to the age of nine, we were in mixed classes, after that, the boys had to move to the boy's school and the girls had girl's only classes after that. It was a wonderful school and we were day scholars once more; which was nice, but it wasn't without its problems, my sister Janet was always getting into trouble with the big girls by telling tales on them. At play time or during lunch break they would come looking for her and she would come to me for protection and although I did not mind hitting her myself, I would not let anyone else do it. This meant I was always on the receiving end because those girls were bigger than me.

We had to walk a couple of miles to school and back every day and the short cut was through a dirt track, we used to call it the mud road. In the monsoon season it used to get churned up by the bullock carts so you had to negotiate it very carefully or get stuck, ankle deep in the mud; I lost a shoe once in the deep mud and never found it again and had to go home with one shoe.

Being day scholars we had to provide our own lunch, so the Thai (a young servant girl employed to help the ayah and look after us children) used to bring our lunch up to us in a Tiffin carrier. This was a container consisting of about four pans that fitted into each other, the first one would hold boiling water or charcoal to keep the food hot, the next would hold the rice, the next the curry and the last the sweet and on top of all that, would be plates and cutlery, wrapped in a large napkin and carried on her head.

I don't know if she came to us first or to my brother, but that was one of her duties.

The teachers were mostly very nice, but not all. There was a Mrs. Duggan, a rather large lady with hands the size of dinner plates and when she slapped you across the face, your brains literally shook. If I went home with hand prints on my face, I had to explain how it got there. I would get another good hiding for getting into trouble in the first place. Then there was Miss Wheeler who became Mrs. Lawless, that name suited her better. She had a violent temper and if she did not have your undivided attention, she would throw anything that came to hand at you, even the wooden backed chalk erasers. If she thought you were nodding off or yawning, she would push a stick of chalk in your mouth.

The head mistress, Miss Watson, was a lovely lady and as I was always in trouble for answering back, I was always in detention which meant I had to come to school on Saturday morning and sit in the headmistress's office till lunch time. One day she said to me, "Patricia, can't you be a good girl? Just once and we can both have Saturday off". Then there was Madame Cesay, she was the French mistress. I was never very attentive; so as soon as she arrived, she would say to me "Go to ze back of ze class, you naughty Mickey Mouse, I am not teaching you." The problem was; I was easily distracted; we had very high skylights in the classrooms and sometimes the monkeys that lived in the school grounds would jump on the skylight and I used to pull on the cords and give them a ride.

It was the practice at the school that the children remained in their class and the teachers moved from class to class with their different subjects. Also at the end of the year exams, you only went up a class if you passed your exams, if you did not you had to stay in the same class for another year. So sometimes you had sixteen year olds in the same class as ten year olds because they had failed six years in a row.

I was very good at sports and used to win all the races, but I did not do myself any favours by being better than every one else in my age group. The teachers thought it would be a good idea to put me with the bigger girls and of course I didn't stand a chance against the big girls, so I lost heart.

Life was back to normal. Well, normal for us anyway. Father was not in our lives and we had nothing to fear. We went shopping with nana once a month when she got her pension. She would treat us to lunch in a restaurant and tea in a special shop, where they sold cakes called butter beans, it was a kind of choux pastry filled with cream and iced. That was our monthly treat. At other times we would go to town with Mum to buy hard goods, as she called it.

We would go to an agent, who hired out young boys and girls not much older than ourselves. They had a licence number which they handed over to my mother, they would have a huge basket on their head and they would have to follow us everywhere we went and whatever we bought was put into the basket. When the basket was full, we went home by bus or taxi and the poor child had to walk miles to our address before he or she got paid and had their licence returned. They then had to give the money to their owner and probably got paid a pittance. On a few occasions, if there was rather a lot of shopping to deliver, my mother would feel sorry for them and pay their bus fare, but they would have to walk back. We had no idea how awful we were to the natives until we came to this country. It was just how things were.

We were not allowed to socialise with any Indians, it was frowned upon. It's sad to think that we pick up all our prejudices from our elders.

I recall just how embarrassed we were to have to carry our own shopping when we first came to England; we used to hold the shopping bags behind us so nobody could see that we were carrying shopping; but that's how we were brought up. Gradually, we learned the hard way. We had to do worse things than that; twice a week we had a market in Salisbury, Tuesday and Saturday; when the market closed for the day, we children would have to go to the fruit stalls and ask if we could have the wooden boxes that the fruit and vegetables came in; so we could have kindling for the fire. It was all very embarrassing, but we had to do it.

We grew up fast in the first couple of years in England.

Towards the end of 1942, my mother and father got back together again briefly. She became pregnant with my youngest sister Geraldine. It was obviously deliberate to tie my mother down with another baby, because he disappeared once more and did not keep in touch until the baby was born. After he saw the baby, he was off again.

Just before Christmas when Geraldine was about two months old, Mum received a letter saying he had met a missionary family, very nice people he assured us, who would like to give us a holiday for Christmas. So, off we all went, to Mahiem in Bombay. As I have mentioned before, it takes three days and two nights to travel to Bombay from Bangalore by train.

When we arrived, we were introduced to a Mrs Maureen Young. She had an eighteen year old daughter Julie, a fourteen year old daughter, Betty and a son Bertie, about my age. She also had an older son, who was killed in an electrical accident. The slap in the face came, when it was time for bed; we were informed that mum, us children and, her two youngest children would be sharing the same bedroom; while dad and Mrs. Young would be sharing her bedroom. Julie had moved out to a place of her own because Julie and her mother were sharing my father between them. It seems mum had no option but to stay till after the Christmas holidays; so they both enjoyed humiliating my mother every day.

Maureen liked playing mind games; her favourite game was to ask us every evening after my father came home. "Do you love your aunty Maureen" She would ask, she always asked Janet first, Janet would reply, "yes aunty Maureen I do love you" Then she would ask Denzil; "Denzil darling, do you love your aunty Maureen" and he would grunt umm she would turn to me and repeat the words, She always left me to the last to get the best results and I always replied "no I don't". Then dad would take off his belt, march me down the corridor, undress me and tried to beat me into submission. This happened every evening while we were there. That's when I hated my sister most of all because I felt she was being disloyal to my mum and mum was in the room while we were being asked. Mrs Young did not like me and I did not like her and it showed. One evening mum said to me; "why don't you say yes and save yourself a beating;" "well I don't like her and I'm not going to say I do", I replied.

On one occasion when her ayah had a day off, she had to do the cooking herself, so she told us to line up with our dinner plates in the kitchen so she could serve us and we could carry our own meals to the dining room. When it came to my turn, I tripped and fell, the plate broke and she went mad. "You've broken my best dinner plate" she said, "Your father, bought it for me he's going to be furious". After looking at my mother's face, she calmed down and said, "Never mind, we'll put it in the bin, so he won't know anything, about it". The first words she uttered when my father walked in the door were; "your daughter has broken my best dinner plate"; off I was marched to receive my punishment; when my mother said to her, "if you don't put a stop to this, I will pull every hair out of your head; she came running up saying "Jim, Jim, please don't hit her", so mum saved the day.

Christmas day arrived, we were very excited when we unwrapped our presents. I remember I had a beautiful German doll. It was jointed, at the elbows, wrists, knees and ankles. I had never seen a doll like it before, or since. It had blond hair and beautiful clothes. Janet had a lovely, dusky skinned doll dressed as a Hawaiian with a grass skirt and flowers and jet black hair. It was made of china. My brother got a train set.

After lunch, we children went for a walk in the near-by park; we girls took our dolls with us. There was a low wall surrounding the park; my sister Janet decided to walk on the wall, she fell off and the doll smashed. She was really scared that she would be in big trouble as she only had the doll a few hours.

About a week later, we all went to the beach which was only a few hundred yards from the apartment. Mother sat on the beach with the baby and Janet while my father my brother and I went into the sea. My father decided to play some more of his mind games, so he took my brother a long way out of his depth and left him there. My brother could not swim and was struggling to keep afloat. My mother was screaming to Dad to bring him back, so he eventually got to him before he went under for the third time. He then turned his attention to me, he took me out to the depth of his armpits, took me by my legs and placed me upside down between his legs and held me there. My lungs were bursting, I could not breathe, and my mother was having hysterics on the beach. I thought I was going to drown. I don't know how I thought of it but I sank my teeth into his calf, hard. He was so shocked, he released his hold and I got away back to the beach.

Thankfully the holiday was over and we went back to Bangalore, back to Nana. When we got back to Bangalore; we had to move out of our ten Rupee home and move in with nana, possibly because dad had cut mum's allowance yet again, now he had two families to support. He still paid our school fees though because we still went to Baldwin's school. Later that year in the summer of 1944 we were told dad was coming for a visit; we were terrified; because all the trauma in our lives we all did badly in our exams, none of us had ever been held back before and we knew we would be punished so we decided to run away from home. We planned for weeks ahead we spent all our pocket money on things like tea, coffee, sugar and things we thought we might need to survive; we raided the medicine cupboard for plasters, iodine and disinfectant. We were going to live in a disused monkey house, in Victoria park, the Indian name was Lal Bargh, it was acres of parkland and once boasted a small zoo which was no longer in use, there was a statue of Queen Victoria at the entrance. It was also famous for a structure called Tipu's Look Out. Tipu was a sultan in Victoria's reign, who hated the British; he had a bad reputation for his cruelty to his British prisoners. It was at this location that he was supposedly captured.

Just before Dad was due to arrive my grandmother decided to have a spring clean. She got the servants busy, they cleaned from top to toe, and they also discovered our hidden supplies. When we got home from school, Nana had it all laid out on the table and demanded to know what it was all about. Everything was confiscated and we all got a good hiding and another one from Dad when he got there. He stayed a few days, and then he was off again. He visited again the following year and we never saw him again until we were grown up. He had left the army and joined the merchant navy. He also stopped providing for his family and as we had no money of our own, my mother for the first time since she was married had to find work, so she joined the W.A.C.I. (the women's army) and worked as a secretary in the ration's department.

We were very lucky for her to be in this position. It meant that we never went without anything; she arranged with customers to trade rations she didn't want with things they didn't want. As she was now army personnel, we met a lot of army families; Mum became a social butterfly. She was never home; she had a wardrobe full of evening gowns, had her hair done in a new style every day and went dancing every night. If my Nana refused to baby sit or she could not get the ayah to stay the night, she would get us all dressed up and take us along with her; no one was going to make her miss her dancing. As it usually didn't finish till past midnight, we children would fall asleep in our chairs; we still had to go to school the next morning. Normally, she could not stand us being around. If she wanted to get rid of us, she would give us money and say "why don't you go to the pictures? Or, here's some money, go and hire a bicycle and take your little sisters with you". My brother and myself used to hire boys' bicycles because of the crossbar, Janet used to sit on Denzil's crossbar and Gerry would sit on mine and we would be gone for hours and we went to the cinema about three times a week, so we saw a lot of films. Even before she started work, she was never home, she was always in someone else's house; every meal time, my nana would say to us children; go and find your mother, tell her it's lunch time or tea time, or whatever it was and we children would go from house to house asking if my mummy was there, nana said come home.

I was always made to play with Janet, although I hated playing with her; no matter what went wrong or if she fell over, she would go running in to mum saying Patsy, as they used to call me, did it on purpose, then I would get a good hiding. I always got my revenge, on the way to school the next morning; she wouldn't make a sound until we got to our gate at four o'clock in the evening, then she would scream and cry, as though I had only just done it; needless to say I would be given another beating I never learned. Sometimes when I was made to play with her, we would play at dressing up and I made sure she was always the boy, I would dress her in my brother's old clothes and I would always be the bride or the princess, dressed in my mother's petticoat with a net curtain on my head.

Mum met a sergeant called Sidney Newman and started an affair; she really fell for him in a big way. He was very nice to us but we didn't know he was married. We were invited to all the camp functions including the swimming pool on Sundays. They had an Olympic size pool with three diving boards; they also had a dinghy in the pool to take the children for a ride round the pool. That is how I learned to swim, by accident, I was hanging on to the back of the dinghy letting it pull me around when Mum spotted me and shouted for me to let go so I did, and realised I was in the deep end. It was sink or swim, so I swam and frightened everyone.

In 1946, when the Japanese war was over, the prisoners of war came home. A lot of them were in a bad way; they were sent to a military hospital in a place called Dulali, (I'm not sure, of the way it is spelt). The army needed nurses and as my mother was a nurse before she was married. She volunteered and was sent away for six weeks to nurse them until they were sent back to Britain. She came home with some real horror stories about what she had seen.

Our way of life in India I suppose, would be considered a pretty easy life style. We never wanted for anything material, we had more than enough to eat, in fact I could say, we were very wasteful. Luckily, the servants could take home what we didn't want for their families. There were no such things as refrigerators in those days, so everything had to be made fresh every day. The ayah had to go to the meat market every day to buy whatever meat my nana asked for; beef lamb, pork, or any other meat she wanted. If she wanted chicken, my nana would buy several live chickens and keep them in the yard to fatten them up and kill them when she needed them. Meanwhile, we children would make pets of the chickens and even name them and when it came time for nana to select one or two for a meal, we children would cry and say, no nana, not Daisy or Betty or whatever we had named them. She would then say, don't be silly that's what they are there for and she would wring their necks; then we would refuse to eat them.

Apart from what my mother called hard goods, everything else was brought to the door. The egg man brought a huge basket of eggs on his head and put it down on the verandah; nana would bring a bowl of water, choose the eggs she wanted and put them in the water. If they stayed at the bottom of the bowl she would buy them, if they stood up on end they were bad, and the man had to take them back.

We went to the cobblers to have our shoes hand made. If we needed new clothes, mother would buy bolts of material in whatever colour and whatever fabric she wanted. She would then send for the tailor, who would arrive with his sewing machine on his head. He would sit on our verandah. After accepting his price, mother would tell him what she wanted, or show him a picture of what she wanted, he would take measurements and without even a pattern he would turn out beautiful clothes.

You hardly had to go out for anything, the greengrocer came to the door and you hand picked everything and Nana was very fussy. The ice cream man came round, also the sweetmeat man. In the summer, late in the evening they used to sell something called ice apples. They were very strange, semi transparent fruit of the Palmira tree, very cooling. Each vendor called out their wares; it was the only way you knew they were about. Sometimes the air was full of the sounds of different vendors calling out their wares.

The dhobi used to come round once a week. Nana kept a book with a check list. He used to come into the house, spread a used sheet on the floor; the dirty washing would be counted and entered in her book, tied in a bundle and taken away to be washed. Likewise when the washing was brought back it was all counted and checked against her book and heaven help the dhobi who lost anything.

There were Chinese vendors that used to come round on bicycles, the same way we get French onion sellers in this country; only they used to sell haberdashery. They would come into the house and lay out all their trays of buttons, ribbons, lace, elastic, sewing needles and anything the housewife may need. We used to call them Chinese John's; we called all of them John. I have no idea why, but my Nana would say if you see a Chinese John anywhere while you are out playing would you tell him to call because I need a few things.

Every morning a woman would arrive, sit on the corner of the street and make breakfast for anyone who wanted it. She made something called oppers or hoppers, I can't rightly remember. I have a feeling they were made from rice flour, you could have egg oppers or milk oppers or something called iddy oppers, those were all stringy. I don't know how they were made, but they were all delicious. If anybody didn't feel like making breakfast, they would go and see the opper woman.

My grandmother was very keen on keeping us healthy. Every morning we were given a large spoonful of cod liver oil. We would queue up with our spoons and if she was too busy at the time to notice we would take it out into the garden and tip it on the plantain trees. We must have had the healthiest plantain trees in India. She also deemed it was important to be purged once a week, so every Saturday we were given either castor oil or Epsom salts. Yuk! When she discovered we were not taking our cod liver oil, she bought cod liver oil and malt instead. We did not mind that. So, we had a desert spoon full every morning.

On the whole we were pretty healthy, we had all the usual childhood ailments, like measles, mumps, chicken pox and the like. We used to regularly get something called sore eyes; it's caused by a particular fly. It makes your eyes pussy and your lids stick together. I think it can cause long term damage if it goes untreated. The only serious illness I had was dysentery and had a long stay in hospital with that. Also my brother Denzil was in hospital suffering from paratyphoid which was very serious at the time.

Every year we used to have to be vaccinated or inoculated against something or the other, it was compulsory. We used to queue outside the headmistress's office and in turn go in and get the needle or the wheel, I still have the scars to this day.

Sunday was a ritual; we would have to go to church at eight in the morning with Nana to All Saints church. When we got home we had breakfast and went to Sunday school at Mr and Mrs Marriot's, at ten. After Sunday school it was lunch or Tiffin, as it was called. Then at two thirty we had to go back to All Saints to their Sunday school and we had to remain immaculate all day. We enjoyed going to Sunday school, it was better than doing homework. After Sunday school at church, we three older children had to walk around our small town in our Sunday best. I'm not too sure of the purpose, but I think it was to show off to the neighbours.

Our vicar, Reverend Stephens, was one of those strict disciplinarians and he stood no nonsense from young or old. He would not think twice about admonishing anyone in public. On one occasion during Sunday Communion service my brother Denzil, my sister Janet and myself (none of us were very old at the time) were watching the people taking communion and wondering what was taking place. My brother was trying to explain by going through the motions. All this did not go unnoticed and as we left the church Rev. Stephens stopped my grandmother at the door and in front of everybody told my grandmother off. He told her that if we could not behave, she was not to bring us anymore. She was totally humiliated and furthermore very angry with us. I think we were not allowed to go to church for a couple of weeks.

Once a year during one of the Hindu festivals, we would go out and watch Tiger Dancing (not real tigers). They were men with their skin painted like tigers; they wore tight short pants of tiger or leopard skin and caps or the real heads of the same. There would be about a half a dozen of them, also a hunter, or shikari, he was dressed in European safari clothes and a pith helmet brandishing a rifle. He would pretend to shoot the tigers. The men dressed as tigers carried whips and chains and used to lash their own bodies. They could be bleeding, but they never seemed to feel it, it was as though they were in a trance. I was told they beat themselves to atone for their sins. Whatever the reason, it was all very exciting and scary. Sometimes although we were forbidden to, we would follow them back to their villages, which was a long way away from our town. Then we would have to find our way back. Then there was the festival of light or Diwali, where every Hindu household had lighted candles, indoors and out; it was very pretty, with hundreds of floating candles.

Also there were the sounds we would wake up to, the sound of horns, conch shell, I think! It was something to do with the Hindu religion. Then the religious leaders, of the Muslims, calling the faithful to prayer, from their minarets. The nights were very noisy with the sounds of insects, frogs croaking, crickets chirping, the occasional howling of Jackal's as they prowled through the streets scavenging for food.

There was no twilight, as we know it; the part of India where we lived; about seven p.m. it goes from daylight to dark, like a curtain being slowly drawn. The darkness would be punctured by hundreds of little lights darting in and out of the branches of the trees; those were fire flies. We often watched from the verandah.

The insect life is not something I miss. There were red ants, black ants, termites or white ants, bully ants; Those were huge ants with large heads and huge pincers and when they sunk their pincers into you nothing could make them let go, not even if you killed them and knocked their bodies off, the heads would remain still embedded in your skin. Then there were spiders, scorpions, giant centipedes, all with a sting, not necessarily fatal, but could make you quite ill. There were bed bugs and cockroaches, mosquitoes and lots of other creepy crawlies. It was a running battle to control all these things.

We used to put the legs of the beds and cupboards standing in small round tins of kerosene oil so anything that could not fly would be deterred from crawling up into the clothes or food. We had mosquito nets to stop them making a meal of us during the night. If we were restless and disturbed the net, and left a hole for the mosquitoes to come in, the next morning we would be covered in bites where they feasted on our blood.

Then there were the flies, awful flies. They used to swarm on every thing. Everything had to be kept covered at all times. There were small lizards, I don't know their proper name, but we used to call them flycatchers, they used to live in the house, usually on the ceiling. They made a strange ticking sound. They were quite harmless, except to the flies. When a fly settled on the ceiling, the flycatcher's long tongue would unfurl and the fly would be gone in a flash, quicker than the eye could see.

There were mice, rats and some rodents called bandicoots as big as cats, some of them. Then there were snakes, constrictors as well as venomous ones, cobras usually. I believe the cobra was one of many Hindu deities, but snake charmers used to bring the snakes to people's gardens in baskets and charm the snakes into dancing to the music of their pipes for money. They also brought a mongoose in a bag and when the snakes were out, they would produce the mongoose to fight the cobras almost to the death before they would separate them. A mongoose and a cobra are natural enemies and a mongoose always wins. The cobra did not stand a chance as the charmer always milked the cobra's venom first.

The only beautiful insects were the huge variety of moths and butterflies. Those came in many colours and sizes some as big as a man's hand. There were gigantic dragonflies with glistening, gossamer wings, also grasshoppers, crickets and sometimes, gigantic grasshoppers that might have been locusts. There were also Praying Mantis and huge stick insects, gold beetles, (we used to tie a thread around its head so they could fly while still being a prisoner) and little tiny beetle-like creatures that used to burrow into the sand backwards, you would not believe, just how fast they could move, I believe we used to call them Guinea Pigs I have no idea why.

The bird life was many and varied; the colours had to be seen, to be believed, there were Hoopoes, Golden Orioles, kites, parrots and Vultures; you would find Vultures where ever there was a Tower of Silence,(that was where the Parsee's laid there dead on a grille at the top of the tower, the Vultures ate the bodies and the bones fell through to what was considered to be a holy place).

The Parsees originated in old Persia. So whenever you saw vultures, you knew there was a tower of silence in the area.

Nature is not just beautiful, it can also be cruel. We used to watch kites take other birds in flight and eat them on the wing. We used to try and shoo them away but there was nothing we could do really.

There was a troop of monkeys that lived in the school grounds. They were great thieves, but were quite harmless as long as you did not interfere with them or frighten them. Then they could be quite dangerous. There were also Fruit bats, (flying foxes we used to call them) that used to roost in the date palms.

The flora was also quite different. We had four o'clock flowers which only opened at that time, spider lilies which looked like spiders webs. There were all the other normal flowers like Roses, Chrysanthemums and the like. The trees were vivid colours like Flame of the forest, Bougainvillea and Magnolia. There were Mango trees, Tamarind trees, Lemon, Orange, Pineapples, that were grown as low hedges, something called Jackfruit, these grew on a tall tree and the fruit was like a gigantic green hedgehog and when it was ripe it split and inside were dozens of sweet golden fruits delicious, I can still taste them. There were Papaya trees, Custard apple, and some fruit called Pomeloes which was a citrus, a cross between a large grapefruit and an orange with pink flesh and something called a wood apple. In our ten Rupee bungalow garden, we had a Pomegranate tree, Loganberries and all the aforementioned flowers. In the five rupee block, we had two Guava trees, one red and one white, a clump of Plantain trees. They were called table plantains because they were the size of your fingers and very sweet,(a type of banana).

On the outskirts of the town was an avenue of trees of different sorts and sizes. Some I was able to climb, which was something I was forbidden to do, but if any one said "no, I must not", that is just what I did. The tallest of the trees were a sort of cotton tree. When the large pods were ripe, they would split and fall off the tree and the air would be thick with this white fluffy stuff with little black seeds attached, I think it was kapok. Sometimes we children would collect the pods and take all the stuffing out, I can't remember what for.

Austin Town consisted of two rows of back-to-back ten rupee homes making four rows and seven rows of five rupee homes, making fourteen rows. Behind the avenue of trees was a field called a maidan and beyond that was called a grass farm where the jackals lived. In the middle of the town was a smaller maidan where we children used to play. On the other side was another maidan a lot bigger than the one in the middle; we used it to play football and ride our bikes and anything else that took up a lot of space. On the other side of that were the local shops the barbers, the bicycle hire shop, the native grog shop and beyond that the main road and the bus stop. At the other end of the town near the entrance of one of the Indian villages, was a deep well, it seems it was used when people wanted to commit suicide.

I still remember the postal address of my Nana's five rupee bungalow; it was number thirty seven, block four, Austin Town, Bangalore.

The summer holidays started in the middle of May and ended in the middle of July, as this was the hottest time of the year and if you went out in the middle of the day without your pith helmet on you would end up with sunstroke as I know to my cost. We had two monsoon seasons when it rained for days on end without stopping. There would be flash floods and the roads would be running red mud. On the main roads were storm drains about four feet deep and they would be like a raging river. Both the maidans would flood and all the local children would swim in the red, muddy water.

During the hottest months, when it was too hot to sleep indoors, our beds would be put up in the compound, mosquito nets and all.

It was quite safe as all the bungalows had a six-foot high wall built around the compound, and a gate that bolted from the inside. There was no glass in the windows, just iron bars with wooden shutters that were bolted from the inside at night.

Bangalore is on a plateau, so we had a temperate climate compared to the rest of India. Other parts of India had extreme heat in the summer and extreme cold, even snow, in the winter. Bangalore was referred to as the pensioners' paradise because people tended to retire there. The only time it got cold in the winter was in the evening.

So all in all, it was a nice place to live.

Mum and Dad's wedding, October 1933.

3

One day out of the blue Mum received a letter from my father instructing her to hand us three older children over to his mistress, Maureen Young. So she packed all our belongings and took us to Bombay and handed us over. We were shocked and felt betrayed to think she could give us away so easily. What she didn't tell us was he was not going to support us financially any more if she did not give us up. So she had no choice. When Mum handed us over, she gave the woman all our clothes and shoes, bolts of new material for new clothes and pocket money for us children, all of which were confiscated.

We realised my father was not living there (he was living in England at the time). He had no intentions of coming back to her; it was just another one of his spiteful tricks to get us away from our mother. I was about eleven at the time and we never saw him again until I was seventeen.

We stayed with Maureen for about nine months but it seemed like nine years. In that time our health suffered greatly, we were half starved and neglected; our skin had white patches caused by lack of protein. We were never sent to school because education was not free and she was not going to pay school fees for three more children so our education also suffered. She would not pay for a doctor or dentist, so if anything went wrong, we had to suffer. I had an abscess in my left ear and was in pain, she would do nothing about it, it finally burst and I woke one morning with blood and puss on my pillow; this is probably why I am partially deaf in my left ear. My brother had an abscess on his lower gum and it must have been very painful because he cried and I had never seen him cry before.

Maureen was an arts teacher at the local school and when she went to work in the morning we were locked out of the apartment until she came home from work. The eldest daughter, Julie, did not live with us which, was a pity, as she was the only person who was kind to us. Her younger daughter Betty, worked in an Ostermilk factory and the son Bertie, was still at school. When she went to work; my brother, sister and I were left to roam the streets and the beach all day until it was time to go home. When we got home we were given a meal of dhal and rice; this is all we ever got to eat while we were there. After we had eaten, we had to go to bed; so she and her children could have supper by themselves; we could only imagine what they were having, judging by the lovely smells coming from the kitchen.

At one point she decided to rent one of her rooms to a family with use of the kitchen and bathroom. The family name was Mr and Mrs Carr, a daughter Lorraine and a son Colin who were both teenagers. Mrs Carr felt sorry for us and secretly fed us on thick slices of bread and jam.

We were almost native as Maureen would not allow us to wear our shoes (to make them last longer, I suppose!) One day whilst on our wanderings, we came upon a pretty curly haired little girl in the park with her mother and father, who quite obviously had her in their middle years. She was an only child and very spoiled. We played with the child for a while and the parents asked us if we would do this on a regular basis. We said we would and they took us over the road to a palatial house with a huge nursery in which that child had everything any child could wish for.

My brother, sister and myself decided we were on to a good thing, somewhere to go, shelter and things to do. But she was a very demanding little girl and we soon got bored. One day after several weeks, the mother came into the nursery to find us reading comics instead of playing with their little girl, so she threw us out. So that put paid to our little bolthole.

The part of Bombay where we lived was called Mahiem. There was a park called Shivaji Park just to the left of the apartment. They used to hold cricket matches and other sports in the park. The apartment was only a few hundred yards from the beach so we spent a lot of time there making our own fun, pretending to be sailors or fishermen or walk along the beach for many miles. We had all day to do this. Sometimes if we were allowed to, we would take a moonlight walk along the beach with Lorraine, Colin, and Betty.

The Hindus used to take their dead down into the sea to wash them and then after dark they would take them into the burning ghats, which was an enclosure just off the beach and burn their dead. One night out of curiosity I peeped through a hole in the fence and saw a body sit bolt upright on the funeral pyre and I had nightmares for weeks afterwards.

When Maureen realised my father was never coming back, she wanted to get rid of us, so she wrote to my grandmother and told her if she or my mother did not come and get us, we were to be put in a home.

Mum was not able to pick us up because she was up north in Lahore with her sister, it took seven days and nights by train and it was too dangerous to travel as the Hindus and Muslims were fighting each other in the north. It was not quite so bad in the south. Anyway, my grandmother who only had a pension, to live on, spent most of it on train fares to come and get us. She was appalled at the sight of us.

When she got us home, it was evident, she was not able to afford to feed us, for long; so much against her will she put us in an orphanage; I was by now, twelve years old; it was 1947.

After Nana took us back to Bangalore, it took a few weeks, to fatten us up and make us strong enough to face a new era in our lives. My sister and I were taken to an orphanage called, Copalias School for girls. My brother was taken to a church orphanage for boys. We were allowed to go home to Nana once a month for the weekend, when she would feed us all the nice things that we were not getting at school. Because we were not used to the kind of food that they fed us on, my sister and I, starved ourselves for the first three or four days and we could not understand why the other children would fight over our untouched food. We soon learned you either ate what was put in front of you, or you starved. The first night we were there, my sister and I had to share a bed; during the night my sister was sick and I was made to clean it up, it was the hardest thing I ever had to do; to this day I cannot bear to do this task.

The main meal consisted of one Ragi ball about the size of a cricket ball made from black flour and cooked like a dumpling, served with curry of some kind. We did not like it, but we soon learned to eat it.

The matron, Mrs Rodgers, was very strict but very kind as long as you made the effort to fit in. She had a teenage daughter, I don't remember her name, but she took me under her wing. The daughter had a small apartment next to our dormitory and I was always invited in. She was obsessed with trying to make her skin lighter, she had dozens, of different preparations that she used to cover her face and arms with, then she would ask me if she looked whiter and of course I would say yes just to keep in her good books; actually, they made no difference at all.

Mrs Rogers was a very thin gaunt lady, with short bobbed hair and steel rimmed glasses, she looked very forbidding but actually, she was really nice. I think she had a grown up son, but I can't remember a Mr. Rodgers.

The Methodist Church ran the school and the church was next door. I was in the choir and had to go to choir practice once or twice a week. All week we had to wear a drab, grey blue dress but on Sundays when we went to church, we wore white skirts and blouses. As soon as church was finished, we had to change back into our dresses. Saturdays were always very busy; we were split into groups, one group was sent into the playing field with hoes to remove every weed another group to change all the linen and scrub the dormitory floors. Another group had to clean the bathroom, including climbing into a massive steel water heater to de-scale it. I was once almost electrocuted when a silly girl decided to switch on while I was still inside. I don't know how I managed to jump clear as the drum was almost as tall as I was. The rest had to go into the inner courtyard and de-louse each other. I still itch at the thought of it.

Once a week we had to go to the sewing room, where we had to mend anything that was torn clothes, sheets, anything to make things last longer.

Sunday was a day of rest, when we could have visitors or write letters if we had anyone to write to I had a very good friend, Crystal St. Martin. She was from the posh school that we used to attend; she never looked down her nose at us for going down in the world as many of our other friends did. She, and her sister Betty, used to visit often and bring us gifts. I often wonder where she is now.

We had a beautiful tennis court, which we also had to keep weed free. Important people used to come and play and we used to be allowed to be ball girls and get paid for it. It was the only way we could earn pocket money; not that we could go anywhere to spend it. At the other side of the inner courtyard, was a house with a barred window, overlooking the courtyard. We would take our money to the window and call out. The lady of the house would ask us what we wanted, we handed over our money and told her what we wanted, usually condensed milk. When she got what we wanted, we made a couple of holes in the tin and drank it straight from the tin. We learned a lot of folk songs, mostly of German origin and I still remember most of them.

It was 1947 and we had our sports day and were competing against all the local schools. This meant meeting up with all the children from our old schools. My poor brother was most embarrassed and I wanted the ground to open and swallow me up. We were made fun of by our old school friends about our orphan's uniform, all except my friend Crystal, who told them off. It was a day I will never forget.

In November of that year, the then Princess Elizabeth got married to Prince Phillip. The matron allowed us to listen to the wedding on the radio; we sat under her window, outside her office, it was most exciting.

That Christmas when the matron and her family went on leave, we were left in the care of some lady benefactor, who obviously had no idea how to run an orphanage. We thought we had died and gone to heaven. We were fed like kings and the ayah, who did the cooking, was outraged at the extravagance, but she was told to mind her own business and cook what she was told to. We were also taken on trips and picnics. We had a lovely time while matron was away, so it came very hard to get back to routine when she came back.

The following year, 1948, I was thirteen; we heard that mother was coming back to Bangalore from Lahore. She had got a special pass and she felt it was now safe to travel. My aunt, mother's sister Margaret, had given her a lot of money to keep us all going till we sailed to England. Apparently arrangements had already been made, but she foolishly kept all the money together and let people on the train see it. As soon as she fell asleep, they slit open her suitcase and stole all the money. They used to be great thieves in India. Anyway she arrived in tears and destitute. As it took seven days and nights to travel from Lahore to Bangalore, she could not do anything about it en-route because she was afraid she might get killed on the train. Luckily, her sister was well off. And when mother wired her about the problem she sent mother some more.

We stayed at the orphanage till the end of June; then mum got us out in time to prepare us for the journey to England, warm clothes to be made also new shoes to be made, vaccinations and medicals to arrange; it was quite a busy month.

Then came the day we had to go to Bombay to the embarkation camp, it was all very exciting. Mum was given free passage as she was in the women's force until she was demobbed, but someone made a mistake about her rank and sent us to the officers' camp. Although she told them of their mistake, they left us there and the mistake was continued all through the trip. We had officer's cabins and ate in the officer's dining room and had wonderful steward service. We did not have to rough it like the other ranks. We sailed from Bombay on the twenty-first of July on board the S.S.Ormond from the P&O Line. We had a very rough passage in the Indian Ocean. The waves, were over fifty feet high, they used to crash over the top deck and would leave flying fish stranded on deck. People all around us would be very sick. I think I was one of very few people who was, not sick. The whole of my three weeks on board were wonderful. When we got as far as the Suez Canal, the sea was calm and the weather was hot. All the cameras were confiscated because there was a war on. We also had to anchor for twelve hours as there was another ship coming the other way and it was not wide enough for two ships to cross.

We first docked at Port Said and then at Aden, where the water was so clear we could see huge Rays swimming under the ship. They looked like they were flying. Then we passed the Rock of Gibraltar and watched the White Cliffs of Dover come into view then we docked at Tilbury and what a shock that was.

We docked at Tilbury at two thirty in the afternoon; on the seventeenth of August; it was dark and smoggy, the street lights were on and the double decker buses also had their lights on; I cried thinking we were going to live in a country where the sun never shone.

Mother's boyfriend, Sidney Newman, a Welsh man met us. They had met in India. We children, hardly knew him, he was in the army and lived at Gordon Barracks in Bulford camp.

We travelled from the ship to Waterloo station by train. It was decided we should have a cup of tea and we were in for a second shock, the cups were without saucers and the teaspoons, were chained to the counter and there was no sugar, quite undrinkable.

We then travelled to Salisbury and from Salisbury to Amesbury by train and from Amesbury to Bulford, by taxi. We were delivered to number 80 Gordon Barracks to stay with my auntie Dulcie, a cousin of my mother; it was she who sponsored us to come into this country.

She had a house full. There was my Uncle Bill, Aunty Irene, their three sons, her brother, Joe, his wife Carol and baby Mary, five of us and herself, daughter Hilary and sons Francis and David over crowded, to say the least.

Aunty Dulcie was married to a Quarter Master Sergeant in the army his name was Frank Sharrock 'Tiger' to his friends. He got the name because he did a bit of boxing. Aunty Dulcie, Aunty Irene and Uncle Joe were brother and sisters. I never liked my Aunty Irene or my Uncle Joe; they seemed to resent us being there. My Aunty Dulcie and Aunty Carol on the other hand were very kind to us. The locals surprisingly were very unkind. They used to call us Sambo or Sabu or Nigger. They asked us if we lived in trees or rode elephants. We expected better from army families, as they had served in India; it wasn't unusual to go home with cut heads because we had been stoned in the street.

About three days after our arrival while waiting for a bus to Salisbury, a woman who had been listening to our conversation came up to us and asked us how long we had been here. When we told her three days, she said, "my how clever of you to learn the language, in three days". We were most insulted as English was our mother tongue and we spoke better English than the English.

A few weeks after our arrival, my Aunty Dulcie was informed, that she and her family were to be posted to Singapore by Christmas, so all of us had to find somewhere else to live. The only place was some derelict huts in an abandoned American army camp in Bulford Fields. A lot of homeless families were doing the same. The huts could be made quite warm and comfortable.

Mother's boyfriend moved in with us; he was horrible, given to moods and could be quite childish. He was a married man and his family, lived in Wales and obviously, knew nothing about my mother.

One day, after getting a letter from home telling him one of his daughters was ill, he and my mother had a row. He lost his temper and took it out on us children. My brother jumped to our defence and with that Sidney beat my brother up pretty badly and tore the shirt off his back. It was November and our first winter in England and freezing cold. But we decided to run away, we had no idea where we were going and as we did not have time to put our overcoats on, we decided to shelter behind the cinema in Gordon barracks. As the evening grew dark and the cold was too much to bear, we found our way back to my aunt who had not yet gone overseas. Finally, we were taken back to my mother. She had thrown Sidney out and we never saw or heard from him again.

We went to school in Durrington for a while, I did not like it. Then the authorities decided that they wanted all the squatters to move out of the army huts. They re-housed some families who had been on the housing list the longest and the rest had to move elsewhere. The only option we were given was the workhouse (Tower House) in Salisbury. It was a grim place and certainly not for children. My mother, myself and my two sisters had to sleep in a dormitory with a lot of old ladies who were coughing and groaning all night, it was very scary and my poor brother was put in a dormitory with a lot of old men, a couple of them died on the first night, that really frightened him.

We spent Christmas there, the nurses made it as happy a time as possible for us but it was still a scary place.

We discovered that at the other end of Tower House were some empty buildings, across the road from Newbridge Hospital, which was also empty at that time. With a bit of persuasion, they allowed us and a few other families in our position to move in. We had one floor each, but we were not allowed to cook our own food. So every mealtime we had a long walk to the kitchens to pick up our food, which mainly consisted of fish. Every day for at least one meal it was fish, fried, boiled, baked or soused oh, and kippers for breakfast, cocoa after supper, tea for breakfast, tea with lunch and everything made in great vats. There were mice and cockroaches running about the place and really off putting to say the least. We had no say in the matter, although we had to pay for everything.

We settled down to a routine, Mum had a part time job in Diffey's café, in Blue Boar Row. My brother went to St Thomas' School for boys, my sister Janet and I, went to St Edmund's School for girls. Geraldine was at that time too young for school. On Sundays we used to go for long walks all the way to Odstock and back, at other times we used to get up to mischief by climbing in through the windows of what once was the American army hospital. It was fully equipped and handed over to Salisbury but was not yet in use. We used to pretend at being nurses and used to say rude things over the phone till one day someone answered. We ran out of there and never went in there again. That place became New Bridge, a geriatric hospital; it no longer exists.

In the spring of 1949, we saw three attractive young ladies walking down from Odstock. They had been to visit their father in hospital, they waved to us and so started a life long friendship. They were Queenie, Dimp and Diana Elliot who lived at 26 College Street. They used to cook Sunday lunch and bring it all the way up to us, they were very kind girls.

1949 was a very eventful year, not one I care to remember. After Mum got fed up with being told what to do and when to do it, she decided to look for some where else to live. One of her workmates, Mrs Overton, offered to rent us a room, but only the girls, my brother had to be boarded elsewhere in Park Street. I felt sorry for him, he was always the one separated from the family.

It did not work out too well, two women in the house and mother needed more money to support all these different households, so she went to an employment agency, called Days and took a live in housekeeper's job, on the understanding that she could take my little sister with her.

She went to work for a Mr. Forbes; he had a beautiful house called The Beeches, near Salisbury. He had the finest of furniture, the best of linen the finest crockery and silverware; everything to make a very comfortable home.

But; he was definitely not normal. Apparently, he was a very clever man; he had a doctorate of some sort and was writing a bibliography on Sir Arthur Conan Doyle. He had a fantastic library, which contained a lot of first editions and he never minded us looking at any of them.

He sometimes never paid my mother's wages for weeks on end, which made things very difficult for my mother. He was a man in his forties, very educated but he had no money of his own. His mother used to pay all his bills but she would never send him cash. All the tradesmen had to send their bills to her and she would pay them. He learned to cheat his mother, by asking the trades people to add a one or a two in front of the actual figure and they would give him the difference.

He had no morals at all.

While Mum, was trying to cope with all this madness and having nowhere else to go, she tried to get the council to house us, to no avail. In the mean time, Mrs Overton decided to make skivvies of my sister Janet and myself. My sister complied and she would sit there mending all their clothes. I, of course, refused. She was so enraged, she threw me out. Unfortunately I was ill at that time, flu, or something, I remember I had a very high temperature. My sister never stood by me; it was a case of self-preservation. I packed my clothes and staggered to the bus station and caught the Southampton bus to go and find my mum in Landford. I did not know if I would be able to stay. Luckily, or unluckily, Mum's boss said yes, and a new nightmare began.

Mother, my sister Geraldine and I shared a bedroom and when we were put to bed on my first night there was a knock on the door and in came, Mr Forbes and sat on the edge of the bed. "Are you a virgin?" he asked. I was an extremely naïve fourteen year old. "No," I said, "only Jesus' mother is a virgin." He then asked my sister the same question. She was only five, she said, "No, silly, my sister told you only Jesus' mother was a virgin." "Oh!" he said "you are both naughty girls". Just then Mum came in and asked him to leave. After he had gone Mum said, always make sure you bolt the door from the inside in future, but she never explained why.

It was the school summer holidays when I arrived, the weather was lovely and there was a beautiful garden in an acre and a half of land with a tennis court; everything that dreams were made of but, he spoiled it because he was so weird. He used to roam about the house and garden stark naked, apart from a pair of black socks. We ate at the same table and he used to snatch food from off our plates if he fancied it. He also used to urinate in the teapot and ask us if we would like another cup of tea. We once found him teaching my little sister the alphabet, in the vilest of forms and drawing dirty pictures to match the letters.

He used to call my mother 'Missus' and on one occasion, he called out to her to fetch him a pair of nail scissors. "Where are you" she asked, "in the bathroom," he replied. When she went in, he was sitting on the edge of the bath naked with his penis tucked under. He said "Look! I'm a lady." She threw the scissors at him and went to see the housing officer to explain that her children were in danger from this man and they still would not help.

Things came to a head one day when I was helping Mum in the kitchen. She was washing up and I was drying and putting the silver away. My back was towards him, so I did not know what he was about to do. He bent down to the floor put his hand between my ankles and came straight up. I was so shocked I swung round and slapped him hard across the face. He did not expect this reaction and became hysterical. My mother grabbed a kitchen knife and threatened him with it. He then ran away into the garden to hide and Mum called the police. They found him hiding behind one of the hedges stark naked. At last they believed us. But they still wouldn't give us a house.

The N.S.P.C.C. took me away and sent me to a girl-guide camp somewhere in Andover. I had a wonderful two weeks with them and later joined them, the St Francis Girl Guides My mother and sisters were given a room with the Elliots, the friends we met while we were staying at Tower House. I moved in with them after I returned from guide camp. I never found out what, if anything happened to Mr Forbes.

While at the Elliots', Geraldine played truant with a little boy from her class. Mother was at work and the rest of us were at school. The headmistress came to see me to ask me why Geraldine was not at her school. We knew she had gone to school, so it was panic stations. We had to contact Mum and my brother and we searched the length and breadth of Salisbury. As a last resort we went to the police station, which was located in Endless Street, and there she was, sitting on the counter, no clothes on, apart from her overcoat, being entertained by the police officers. Apparently she had gone to the river, near the old swimming pool and fallen in. She had the good sense to take off her overcoat before she fell in, but I don't know how she got out, but when she did, she took off all her wet clothes and carried them under her arm. It was a Tuesday, market day and she was found wandering round the market quite oblivious of the fact that she had no clothes on until someone took her to the police station. She was so impressed by the police that forever afterwards she would find any excuse to go and see them.

Just before Christmas 1949 we got our first council house, 76 Winchester Street. It was a three storey, four bedroom house, gas lights, outside toilet, cold water only, tin bath and mice, but it was heaven, because we were all together at last.

We had nothing, but we didn't care. Then one of the branches of the Masons, The Round Table, turned up, with everything we needed. It was mostly second hand, but who cared. My mother was so overwhelmed, she burst into tears. We were then invited to a Christmas party, at the Morrison Hall we had a wonderful time and started the New Year in a place of our own.

4

In the spring of 1950, my brother Denzil, my sister Janet and I; were confirmed at St Edmunds church, by the Bishop of Salisbury.

Geoffrey Goodall was our Rector and a very nice person he was too. He had a wife, an adopted daughter and two sons. He used to run a youth club which we belonged to, though I can't remember how often it was held, but I know we had a lot of fun.

Rationing was still on and as my mother always had to be popular, she would share out our sugar rations, between herself and her relatives; but we her children, were not allowed to have any; we had to have golden syrup in our tea; it used to make the tea look purple but as far as she was concerned, tough, it was for her and her friends. We used to have free school dinners, but at least we ate. After school we would ask mum, "what's for tea?" she would reply, "oh go do yourself an egg" that happened every school day; at the week-end, my brother and I would have to cook. We learned to cook at school and finally taught her, she also learned to make curries, being taught by her sister.

In the May of that year I had my fifteenth birthday; every birthday she would tell me I can't afford to give you anything at the moment, but I will make it up to you as soon as I can afford it but she never did; she always found the money for the others; even on my twenty first, she gave me a card in the shape of a key, with one pound and ten shillings in it; all the others got a dress ring or a signet ring.

I knew I would be leaving school that summer so I had to think about, what I was going to do, when I left.

In the mean time, we were given the chance to earn a bit of money by going potato picking. Only the children who were of school leaving age were allowed to go and the money was good. The farmers would send a lorry to the Salt Lane car park to pick us up. We had to have a packed lunch and something to drink. We had to leave about eight a.m. and brought back about four p.m. The days were very hard, back breaking in fact. We had to follow the tractor or the horses, depending on what the farmers had and fill the sacks provided. We would work until lunch time then stop and have our lunch and start again until it was time to go home. We did this until the harvest was over. We were fit for nothing at the end of it but we felt very rich.

Towards the end of June the Headmistress sent for girls who were leaving and asked if any of us would like a holiday job as she needed six of us to work in a private school for boys. The school was called Greenways, in Codford. The owner was going to turn the school into a holiday hotel from July to the beginning of September. We were to fill in as waitresses, chamber maids and dishwashers in fact general dogs-bodies. The six of us shared one bedroom. I can't remember all their names but I remember a Joan and Daisy and Sylvia. It was hard work but we also had a lot of fun. One of the old boys from the school came to spend a holiday with his parents; I can't remember his name but he was my first school girl crush.

There was a riding school nearby and this boy used to go riding. When he got back he would ask me to look after his riding hat which I did with pleasure. I think he felt the same as I did, although nothing was ever said, but he sometimes stood outside the kitchen window while I was washing up and sing "My Foolish Heart," to me, it was a popular song at the time. It was from a film of the same name starring Susan Hayward and Dana Andrews and made me feel weak at the knees.

We worked for most of the summer holidays. I think we had the last week off. It had been decided that I would go to the Technical College to learn a trade, so I chose tailoring. But when we started we found we had tailoring one morning a week but the rest of the time we did maths, English, science, art, cookery, laundry and housework. It was like being back at school.

The college was situated in Churchfields Road near the railway station. I met a few nice girls there and I must say all the tutors were very helpful. I learned to cook well, learned a lot of useful things about housewifery, but not enough about tailoring.

My problem was money, or rather the lack of it. My mother could not afford to keep me at college; when we had to provide material for sewing or cooking, I had to make do with whatever she could find for me. It was embarrassing and the other girls looked down their noses at me and if that were not enough, when I got home I would have to listen to my mother going on about how much it cost her to keep me in college, when I could be out earning. It was a two year course and I knew I couldn't take another year of this, so at the end of the summer term, I went to see the Head to tell her I wanted to leave. She asked why, when I told her, she sent for my mother and mum denied everything. She said I was leaving because I was lazy. The fact was; most of her money went on cigarettes, she was not going to cut down or give them up for anyone; she made that quite clear.

The Head tried to persuade mum to let me stay but she pretended it was my decision. The Head then sent me for an interview with a local tailor to become an apprentice. His name was Robbins, he was Jewish and he worked me extremely hard for thirty shillings a week, but I did learn a lot about tailoring. After a few months he closed down, I don't know if it was to do with ill health or finance, I only knew I was out of a job.

After that I had many and various jobs. I worked in a high class grocer in the High street called Turners, in the Steam Laundry in St Edmunds Church street. I worked in the laundry for several months and mum also worked there at the time. The forewoman was a spinster and a dragon. She seemed to delight in making my life hell! She found fault with everything I did or said. I told mum I was going to give in my notice. She was not pleased, but agreed with me, that the woman was impossible.

In the early fifties it was an employer's market, so some people did almost anything to keep their jobs and men, especially the older ones, took advantage of that. Two or three tried to take advantage of me and got their faces slapped. It goes without saying I got the sack instantly. One of those places was an electrical shop in Fisherton Street; one was a sweet shop in Winchester Street.

Between the summer of 1951 and the spring of 1954 I had about seven different jobs. The shortest one being a day and a half, that one was as a mothers help to an army officer's wife at Winterbourne Gunner. She had a small boy and a baby girl, they were no trouble at all. My job was to wash nappies, general housework and help to prepare the evening meal. Just as I was about to leave, that first evening, her husband came home. As I was putting my coat on, he said "aren't you going to offer this young lady a cup of tea?" very grudgingly, she agreed. He was very polite and respectful and I thought no more of it.

When I got to work the next morning, she was very quiet and standoffish. We got to lunch time and she could contain herself no longer, "I want you to leave," she said, "and don't come back." "Why have I done something wrong" I asked. "No," she said, "but after you left last night, my husband said you were beautiful, and I can't have that." I was not flattered in fact I was insulted that she should think I would look at her husband who was old enough to be my father. She paid me a day and a half's wages, but refused to pay my stamp for the week, so I had to pay for it myself.

Easter of 1951 found me reading a book in the council grounds. It was a lovely sunny Sunday afternoon; suddenly I noticed a group of young national servicemen hovering around me trying to make conversation. I ignored them and after a while they left, all except one. His name was Eric, he came from Cirencester near Gloucester and he was eighteen years old. He asked if he might see me the following Sunday. I said yes; I hoped that the weather would be fine. The following week I thought I would bring a picnic, I had never had a boyfriend before and I was terrified of what my mother might say. Luck was against me. The next weekend it poured and after lunch I was about to go and meet him, my mother said, "Where do you think you are going in this rain?" So I had to tell her and that he was probably waiting for me and getting wet. To my surprise she said, you had better go and fetch him then; after that, he came every week end and brought his friend Geoff with him.

We were never allowed out by ourselves; whether it was for a walk or to the cinema, one or all the family would accompany us. I had my sixteenth birthday in May and he had his nineteenth in June; in July, he was posted to Germany, and I never heard from him until the end of October. I was broken hearted. When he finally did write, I was so angry, I wrote and told him not to bother again.

By the end of October, I met the man who was to be my husband; we met at a dance on a Saturday, at the Palais, on the Wilton road. The dance was run by a man called Gran Selby; he had a large Air Force moustache and a very capable band, his lead singer, called George, had a beautiful voice.

My brother, my sister Janet and myself, used to go dancing every Saturday night; my poor brother had two left feet and could not dance a step; he was just there to chaperone his sisters; he was so handsome and polite, all the girls would fight over him.

At one of these Saturday dances, a young man asked me to dance; he opened the conversation with," My name is Terry Blake, what's yours; I know everybody else in this room, so I might as well know yours"; he also informed me that he was going to take me home that night; I took an instant dislike to him and made sure I left early, to make sure he didn't follow me home. If only I had listened to my first instincts, it would have saved me from twenty eights of misery; two years engagement and twenty six years of marriage.

The following week he asked me out and I said yes; I had no intentions of keeping the date. I said I would meet him outside the Infirmary where I was working as a live in ward-maid at that time; I took a live in job, to get away from my family, I was very unhappy at the way my mother and two sisters treated me. For instance, Janet and I were supposed to take turns to do the housework; when it was my turn, I would have to do it, or else; when it was Janet's turn, mother would do it for her and if I complained, I would get a good hiding.

If Janet wanted anything of mine, she would just take it, knowing she would not be made to give it back, if I tried to take it back, I would get another beating. One instance was when I treated myself to some dinky curlers; I used to roll my hair up at night because my hair was so straight and as I was working, I wanted to look my age. One night, I came home to find my sister wearing my curlers; "take them off," I said, "I need them", "no" she said, "mum said I could have them", "If you don't take them off I will" I said.

Mum came in and said, "leave her alone, I said she could have them"; "but I paid for them and I need them myself". "Alright Janet" she said, "take them off and give them to me".

She cupped her hands to receive the curlers, she then said; "if Janet can't have them, neither can you", and she put them in the dust bin.

My only revenge was always physical, not that it did me any good, I always got it back with interest from my mother; for some reason she always treated us differently.

I had no intentions of meeting Terry that night, so I watched him pacing up and down in front of the hospital, until he got fed up and left.

I thought that would be the end of it but he did not give up easily and by now I was intrigued; I thought he would not bother again but the next week, he did and after several weeks we were going steady. He tried for a long time to persuade me to have sex with him and I refused, then he asked me to his mother's for Christmas. He knew his family would be going to his aunts and the house would be empty. He tried again and said if I loved him it would be alright. Well, that was the first time and after that he was insatiable, any time and anywhere.

Once he'd had his way with me, he totally disrespected me. He accused me of every man I ever spoke to. I wasn't allowed to dance with anyone else except him. If I accepted a dance with any one else, he would accuse me of going to bed with them. He was allowed to dance with whom he liked, but not me. That set the pattern for what my life was to become. And I blame myself for letting it happen. Even though I was very much in love with him, I never came to like him. I never understood the logic in that. Even after we divorced, I felt nothing but contempt, yet it still took another eight years to get him out of my system.

My husband and I became engaged when I was seventeen and he was twenty one; my mother's reaction was "you make your bed, you lie in it". The engagement lasted two years, and during those two years, he lied and cheated his way throughout our whole courtship.

Whenever I found out about it, I threw his ring back at him, but he always managed to talk me round; I must have been very gullible. The ring itself, was a fake, he led me to believe it was a sapphire with diamonds. It turned out to be a paste dress ring costing £6. I only found out years later when I took it to be repaired when one of the stones fell out.

Life was one big cheat from start to finish. Every Saturday while I was at work, he would trawl all the department stores chatting up all the female assistants and make dates with anyone interested. If he was successful, he would tell me he was going to have an early night as he was tired, then he would take some other girl out. He was caught out, by my sister, who by chance happened to go to the same event. She told me about it, but I would not believe her, I thought she was trying to make trouble as we did not get on in those days.

He was working, for Welworthy's, a piston ring factory at that time. They used to have firm's outings from time to time. I was never invited because he said it was staff only and I believed him, even after we were married. It was only after I joined the firm myself that I discovered he was lying. I never did get to go on one of their outings, because he decided he did not want to go any more. I suppose he did not want to be caught out because he was still dating other women, while I was working, under the same roof. I only found out about that many years later, when a girl he had asked out, told me. Apparently she had noticed that he spent his lunch breaks with me and she wanted to know who I was. "Just a friend," he'd said, and we were, newly-weds, at the time. The name of the girl was, Helen, she was East European and a very nice girl.

Terry and I used to go dancing every Saturday night unless he decided he was too tired. But I did not know he had other plans. The rest of the week, we either stayed in where he and my mother would drink tea and exchange dirty jokes all evening, or else he and my brother would go to the pub for a drink. I was never invited along because I did not drink. He was actually embarrassed to be seen my company because I didn't drink or smoke. If we attended a function together, he made me hold a lighted cigarette in my hand and I had to pretend to smoke it; how pathetic was that, for me to comply with his wishes. After a while I refused to do this and he stopped taking me anywhere that his friends would be.

He was one of life's sheep and was desperate to be popular. There were not many people who actually liked him. Most of them laughed at him behind his back. I was always fighting his battles because I did not like people making fun of him.

I used to have a lot of weird dreams, well nightmares really and quite often they came true. When I was seventeen I had this recurring dream. I dreamed my father was at the front door with a suitcase in his hand. When he opened it, it was full of knives. When I told my mother of my dream, she said, "What do we want to see that bugger for?" When I had the dream twice more, she said, "You have a black tongue, now he's bound to turn up." It was quite soon after that while I was at work, he turned up exactly like my dream. The only difference was that the suitcase was full of presents. My sister Janet brought him to where I was working as a waitress in Jacob's café in Endless Street. I threw myself into his arms and cried, I can't imagine why, when he was such an awful father. Anyway, we started corresponding and I asked if he would give me away at my wedding. Mum was furious but relented. Dad agreed on condition that I invited his wife. I said no; it had to be; on his own, or not at all.

Terry's mother was the classic mother-in-law from hell. From the day we met, she made it perfectly clear that she did not like me. Mind you, I think she would have been the same with any girl. There was never going to be anyone good enough for her son. She was furious when we got engaged and offered him money not to marry me. She told him she would buy him a motor-bike and side-car so he could take her out.

Well, we had this stormy courtship for two years, we then set the date for our wedding for the twentieth of March 1954. It was two months before my nineteenth birthday. Suddenly, his mother started making problems. She told him she was going to die and cried a lot. We had originally planned to redecorate my bedroom and stay at my mother's house. We had papered the walls with blue and white wallpaper, and ordered the bedroom furniture. A week before the wedding, Terry came to see me to say, the wedding was off, unless we went to live with his mother, as she was very upset. Foolishly I agreed. Sometimes I wonder if he was looking for a way out. If he were more honest, maybe it would have saved me from a lot of heartache.

My mother told me she could not afford to pay for the wedding. We said that was fine. I paid for the bridesmaids' dresses. We had four, my sister Janet, my sister Geraldine, Terry's sister Anna and my cousin Mary. They all wore blue and carried muffs. My brother Denzil, paid for my wedding dress and I carried yellow roses.

The two tier cake was made by a Polish friend. My husband and I paid for the food and my brother paid for the drinks. We hired the Halle Hall for the reception and got married in St Edmund's Church.

The wedding was a farce. Because the traffic was bad, being a Saturday, I arrived a quarter of an hour late. Mother-in-law was screaming the church down, saying she was going to die. She said she did not want her son marrying a wog. The vicar was angry with her and told me not to worry. His words were "If she wants to die, let her." My husband turned round and glared at me as I walked down the aisle, which made me nervous. So in the responses instead of "For better, for worse," I said "For bitter, for purse, I did not know then how prophetic those words would be.

It was a cold and windy day, but the sun was shining. We did not have far to go to the reception, just across the churchyard. First we had the usual photographs taken outside the church door and some taken as we walked to the reception. We got there first so we could receive our guests. When every one arrived, his family lined up on one side of the hall and refused to mix with any of my family, with the exception of a few of the younger ones. My husband and I led off the dancing, it was the only dance I had with him, and he spent the rest of the evening flirting with a school girl guest, Jackie. She was brought to sing at the reception and from the body language she was singing just to him. We could not afford a proper honeymoon so we decided to go away, for a couple of days. The first night, we stayed at a pub called The Green Dragon; we were covered in confetti and the hired car, had just married scrawled all over it. It was obvious we were newlyweds. The landlady asked my husband if he would like, single or double beds, you guessed it; he asked for single beds. There were roars of laughter, from the customers, as we went upstairs. The next morning I discovered I had left my brush and comb behind I had forgotten to re pack them, after we went to get ready to go away. We had a row because he blamed me for forgetting them. We finally managed to borrow one, from the chambermaid. The next night we stayed in Bournemouth; we came home the following day to another battle zone. Apparently, my father, who had been allowed to stay the night, along with some other relatives, had been very unfriendly and when he went back to his own home, he wrote an abusive letter to my mother, who was rather upset; so I wrote back and said, if he could not respect my mother, he needn't write again; and he never did.

From the left, Janet, Myself, Denzil and seated Geraldine.

Our Wedding, in 1954. Front row from left: Anna Shaw, my sister-in-law, Mary Beale, my cousin, Geraldine Murray, my sister. Back row: Denzil Murray, my brother, Terence Blake, myself, James Murray, my father and Janet Murray, my sister.

My Children, from the left, Patricia, Jacqueline, John and Carol.

We picked up all our wedding presents and gift cards, so we could write and thank everybody for their gifts. While sorting through the cards, I came across one which read, cheque from Aunty Mags and Uncle Pat. I searched high and low for the cheque, but could not find it, so I wrote to my Aunty and asked her to stop the cheque as it had gone missing. I also asked my mum if she had found it, she said no. I waited a long time to hear from my aunt, but she never did reply. It was many years later, when we invited the family, who lived in Surrey, to one of the children's christenings, that we found out that my mother had cashed the cheque and treated herself to new shoes, hat and handbag, telling her sister she would replace it when we came back off honeymoon. We were also told that every time they visited, they had to pay for parties and things that we had already paid for, because mum had told them she had paid for everything and could not afford it. That sort of put them off coming. And to her dying day, she would not admit to any of it.

We started married life in his mother's house and I was made to know I wasn't welcome, every mealtime, I was told I could only touch anything that was cut for me I was not to touch the loaf or make the tea or anything that she handled. She said she did not like black people and considered me dirty. Her husband was my husband's step father. He said that better people than me worked on the railway stations of Bombay selling tea. I did not take his insults too well and argued all the time. I was working as a hair dresser at the time, Terry was in the Territorial Army and they used to have compulsory weekly meetings and two week manoeuvres once a year. If I came home from work and he wasn't there, I would ask, "Where's Terry?" She would say, "He's out with a blonde," or, "How do I know?" When he returned and I asked him where he had been, he would say I told mum to tell you where I was going.

Mother-in-law suffered with multiple sclerosis, so I tried to be as helpful as possible, but she would have none of it. She would rather crawl up the stairs on her hands and knees to brush the stair carpet, than let me help; then when her husband came home from work, she would complain that I didn't lift a finger to help, then he and I would have another row. While my husband and I were at work, she would crawl up the stairs to our bedroom and remove all his dirty washing to launder them herself. She didn't think I was capable of doing her darling son's laundry.

I used to feel very sorry for my sister-in-law who was a little girl at the time. Her mother used to make her do all the chores that she would not let me do. She was a very likeable little girl and she worshiped the ground her brother walked on.

About three months after we were married, Terry had to do his two weeks manoeuvres with the T.A. So now I was on my own and she made the most of it, humiliating me whenever the chance arose. So I went home to my family most days after work. When I went back to go to bed, I found she had made a cup of cocoa, which I drank. I don't know if she was trying to poison me or not, but I started getting stomach pains and feeling sick. After a week of this, I mentioned it to my mother and she advised me not to drink it, so I threw it away. She noticed this and asked why I wasn't drinking the cocoa. I just said I had a bedtime drink with my family and did not need another. So she stopped making me one, and I got better. I told my husband about it when he came home, but he said it was my imagination.

Soon after that, when I felt I could not take any more I went to see our Rector for a chat. I remembered at the wedding ceremony he had said to me, if you find it too difficult to live with your in-laws come and see me, and I will see what I can do. Well he went to see a family who lived across the way from the church and they said we could rent the two front rooms. The one downstairs was a living room and the one upstairs was a bedroom. They were a lovely old couple, Gran and Granddad Luther. We had to share the facilities. The house was two houses knocked into one which they shared with their daughter and son-in-law, Mr and Mrs Healis and two grand daughters, Margaret and Barbara they were all very kind and friendly.

Anyway, when I had seen the rooms and met the people I went back to my husband and told him I was moving out and he could come or stay as he wished; but I was going, regardless. We had to get a dining suite and a couple of arm chairs and moved in on a Saturday. Unfortunately I had to work that day, so I left it to Terry to organise the move. When I got there, I found my mother-in-law arranging my furniture the way she wanted it. I was so incensed I rearranged it in her presence.

Life was reasonably peaceful for the next three months except, that his cousin Alan used to come around, every Sunday lunchtime and take Terry out for a drink. That in itself was not a problem the problem was he would turn up just as I was about to serve lunch, then they would not be back till about three in the afternoon, and lunch was spoiled. Terry knew the old couple liked to cook first, which meant I could not start cooking till about one o'clock. If I complained and asked," why can't Alan come a bit later," Alan would be sarcastic and belittle Terry and say he was henpecked. One Sunday when Alan was being rude, I retaliated and Terry brought his hand across my face and told me I may not talk to his cousin that way. I never forgave Alan for that. After that, hitting me was a regular occurrence.

He went out every night by himself, leaving me on my own; I still did not believe he was cheating on me; one day I said, I am fed up of staying in by myself, I'm coming with you.

No you are not, he said. So I went upstairs and cut every button off all his suits and shirts. I came down and said, now how are you going out. He sat and cried like a baby. I felt guilty, so I sewed them all back again, but he did not go out that night.

By now, I had just started working for Wellworthy's, where I stayed for two years. There is where I met Helen, one of the girls he had asked out. When she realised he was married, she refused to go out with him, and instead she invited me to her bed-sit in Park Street. As he was never in, I accepted. When he found out where I had been, he flew into a rage. He told me I was never to go there again. He said she was a prostitute and she was always bringing men home. I never thought to ask how he knew all this, but he must have been scared, that she would tell me about him, but she never did, until years later.

One day mum said to me, "I've just received a letter from your ex boyfriend, Eric he would like to pay us a visit, so could I borrow your wedding album, to show him your wedding photographs, In fact, why don't you and Terry come to tea and meet him". When we arrived, Eric was there with a friend of his. It was a very pleasant evening except that Terry sulked and left early I assumed he was off out as usual, so I stayed until late in the evening. Eric and his friend walked me back to my front door. I went upstairs to bed and found Terry sobbing his heart out. He was very unkind to me and accused me of all sorts; and asked why I didn't marry Eric instead.

After that he became more and more violent. After a particular bad beating, our land lady sent for my mother and brother. My mother went for him hammer and tongs and my brother wanted to give him a good hiding but I would not let him. Perhaps I should have, maybe it would have cured him. Our landlady was so angry with him she told him he would have to leave but I could stay. I couldn't stay without him, so we had to find somewhere else to live.

We found two rooms in Ivy Street with Vera Elliot one of the sisters we met in 1949. She was, at one time a lodger at mum's house in Winchester Street, she was now married to Joe Smigelski, he was Polish and she was pregnant with her first baby.

Terry changed his job, he became a fireman on the railway and always came home looking like a coal man. Unfortunately, he had a habit of putting his dirty hands on the white walls as he climbed the stairs, leaving his hand prints all over the walls. This did not please Vera and I can't say I blamed her, but he didn't seem to care.

I had my twenty first, birthday while we were there. My sister Janet bought me the most beautiful black lace cocktail dress as a birthday present. I felt like a queen in it. It must have cost a week's wages.

About that time, my cousin Thelma and husband Lionel and baby Geoffrey, emigrated; to Canada. We decided that we would like to go also. We applied and went to Canada House for an interview, did all the necessary things we were asked to, medicals and the like. Sold our furniture and waited for a sailing date. At the last minute, we received a letter saying they needed papers from my father as proof of my nationality. Unless we had these papers, we could not apply. As we did not know where he was and we were not able, to contact him, that was the end, of that dream. Forever after that, when we had a row, he would blame me for that. He used to get nasty and call me names and saying "Go home Pakistani." I used to get my own back and say to him, "At least I'm not a kangaroo." (He was the illegitimate son of an Australian who was married to his mother's sister.)

We moved in with my mother and two sisters. They had previously moved from Winchester Street to Essex Square in West Harnham. The idea was that as I was now working in the cinema and my mother was working full time, my sister Janet was working at Dunn's Seeds and Geraldine was still at school, that I would do all the cooking and cleaning before I went to work in the afternoon. We would pay no rent, just half the food. Things would have worked out well, except my sister Geraldine was a spoilt brat and she was allowed to do as she pleased. After I had gone to work and left four meals and four puddings, she would eat her meal if she chose to and she ate her pudding and my husband's as well. When I told her off about it, my mother got very spiteful and told us we had to go. Until we find somewhere else, we were not allowed to go through the living room to the kitchen; we had to go out of the front door, round to the back door to use the kitchen, regardless of the weather. If I tried to go through the living room my sister Janet, used to block my way by putting her feet on the wall to stop my going through and I used to have to jump over her legs to get to the kitchen. I was pregnant at the time but did not know it and to be fair, neither did Janet, but it did not excuse her behaviour. We found a place, by the end of October 1956.

Our next move was to a caravan site on the Southampton Road which we rented from the site owner's it was hardly big enough to swing a cat. It was October and very cold. The only heat came from an oil fired heater and occasionally, when the wick burned low, it would smoke the place out and blacken all the walls. I was still working at the cinema; there were no buses that ran to fit in with my timetable, so I had to walk a couple of miles to and from work. Terry owned a Lambretta, but he would not give me a lift home. He would follow me at a distance and let me walk, although he knew I had been on my feet all afternoon and evening. I really don't know what he hoped to see.

After I saw the doctor and he confirmed the pregnancy, I was over the moon, but a few weeks later, I started to bleed. The doctor sent me to bed and told me I had to stay there for three weeks or I might lose the baby. By now it was December 1956. Four days before Christmas I haemorrhaged. I remember it was a quarter to seven in the evening, the Archers had just come on the radio and my bed was a sea of red. I was on my own and very scared. Just then Terry came home from work, he took one look at me and flew down the road to the nearest telephone box and sent for the ambulance. I spent a very painful night. They told me I was four months pregnant and the baby was too big, to abort its' self, so they had to remove it. The following day they did a D and C. and I had to spend Christmas in hospital.

When I was fit enough, I went back to work. The doctor said try again in about three months. When the three months were up I suggested to my husband, that we try again. He said no. When I asked why, he said "if you have a baby, I'll be neglected". But I did persuade him and on the thirteenth of January 1958, my eldest daughter Carol was born. I went into labour at one thirty in the morning. My husband sent for the ambulance about four o' clock, he didn't even accompany me to the hospital and Carol arrived at eleven. For the next ten days at visiting time for fathers he would come and sit by my bed, read the paper that he'd brought with him, ignore me most of the time and frequently look at his watch to see if was time for him to leave. To add insult to injury, when it was time for me to go home, he sent his cousin Alan to pick me up.

We left the rented caravan and bought one of our own; the caravan was second hand but it was luxury, compared to the one we rented. We rented some land behind the White Horse in Quidhampton.

On my first night home with the new baby, instead of spending time with me, he and my brother who was home from the Merchant Navy, chose to spend the evening in the pub. They came back about ten o'clock, bringing two women with them. They didn't even know the women; they said they had come to see the baby. I was angry and embarrassed as I was breast-feeding at the time.

Actually it's a miracle she was ever born. When I was in my eighth month we were having lots of rows, usually about his selfishness and neglect of me. I told him if I meant so little to him, I was going to go across the road and put myself on the railway line. He said go on then. I was by now hysterical and walked out of the caravan. He followed me out and punched me hard in the stomach I thought I would surely lose the baby. Luckily, everything turned out fine.

He then decided to become a painter and decorator. He took a course at the technical college and when he learned enough about it, he went to work for a firm who were painting aircraft hangars. He would come home every night and be sick from fear of heights. I used to feel sorry for him, but he wanted to better himself and I admired that. But he refused to grow up and be a responsible human being. He was always borrowing money from his mother or my mother and he would tell them it was for me. I didn't know about it till they asked me to return their money. His mother also kept him in cigarettes until he was about forty years old.

There was a little shop in the village, which also served as a post office. I often shopped there for odds and ends until one day the lady who ran the shop said she could no longer serve me till all the money my husband owed was paid back. She said my husband owed several pounds for cigarettes he had bought on credit. I was very embarrassed. It took some time, but I paid it all back. I asked her not to give him credit ever again and he was furious with me for embarrassing him.

By the time my daughter was six months old, we were in so much financial trouble that he told me I had to get myself a job. I did not like the idea of leaving a small baby, but he was adamant. So I had to wean the baby off the breast and on to the bottle thinking he was going to look after her himself, but he had other ideas. He used to wheel the baby down to his mother who lived a few yards down the road from us and fetch her back just before I got home. I got myself a job, working five evenings a week in the nurses dining room for twenty hours a week and on occasions, when the doctors had a social do, I was expected to work at the weekend. That wasn't very often, thank goodness. At these dinner parties, the menu would be extensive and varied. The chef would say to us girls who were waitresses for the evening that we could have anything on the menu for your supper after the guests have had theirs. I decided to try pheasant in wine, as I had never tasted pheasant before; the outcome was that I was very sick all night. To my husband, it meant that something unsavoury had been going on, so I was punished with accusations and sulks. He had a happy knack of twisting anything you said to his advantage.

I noticed that my daughter was always poorly with a cold and a temperature. It was autumn, but we had a very snug caravan, so I could not understand why this should be. One evening when I got home from work, I found the caravan empty. So I went to his mother's to find out what was wrong. I found the baby and pram with his mother. It was pretty foggy that night. I realised then why she was always ill and gave in my notice. I refused to go out to work until the baby was older.

Once my family found out I was pregnant, they decided to make it up with me; they made a great fuss of the baby and allowed us to hold the christening party at their house. Soon after that Janet met her first husband Brian, I think they met at a ballroom dancing class. I never really trusted him; they got married, when my daughter Carol, was about nine months old.

Terry was an expert at destroying me with his cruel tongue. I had put on a bit of weight after having my daughter and feeling less than glamorous. So I thought I would do something to get him to take a bit of notice of me. I had a rather smart black suit that I had bought to wear as a going away outfit. Well, it no longer fitted, so I sold it to my sister and with the money she gave me, I decided to buy myself a beautiful sexy nightdress It was a flame-coloured see-through creation that I bought at M&S and I thought I looked wonderful in it. That night I put it on and said to him, "what do you think"? He looked at me and said; "if you had a figure like Marilyn Monroe, maybe, but on you it's a waste". It took the wind out of my sails completely.

By now I was pregnant with my second daughter and in October of 1958,

I miscarried. The doctor came and said it's all over, everything has come away. But a few weeks later, I went back to the doctor and told him I was still pregnant. "Rubbish he said, I assure you, you have lost the baby". He examined me anyway and said "you are right. It must have been one of a twin and you must take care of yourself". Jacqueline was born on the fifth of May 1959, she was the strangest looking baby; she was the smallest in weight but longer than the others; her skin was a shade of purple and she had dark curly hair. She also had extra eye lashes growing, along the side of the normal ones; I was quite concerned at the time, but I needn't have worried the extra ones fell off with time.

When I was in hospital, having my second daughter, Janet looked after Carol; it was good practice as she was by now pregnant with her first baby.

My best friends, Ann and Harry Glover.

6

I met my best friend, Ann Creed, when I became an apprentice hairdresser for Mr Peters; in Devizes Road in Salisbury. As an apprentice one has to do all the dog's-body jobs like cleaning, dusting, shampooing, etc. I decided I did not like Ann at all, she was extremely bossy and found fault with everything I did. She also used to run her fingers over everything I had dusted; I became quite nervous and started dropping things in my attempt to please; but I did learn a lot from her and gradually we became the best of friends. This was in 1953 and after nearly sixty years later we are still the best of friends. I am Godmother to her children and she is Godmother to mine.

She met and married Harry Glover about a year after I married Terry and in the early years we used to go out in a foursome. Harry was great fun, he has a wicked sense of humour and I never quite knew how to take him. My husband always had to spoil our outings with his jealous suspicions. He did not say a word, while we were out, but when we got home he would fly into a rage and accuse me of having an affair with Harry. Ann could not stand the sight of Terry and couldn't understand what I saw in him. She only tolerated him for my sake.

The hairdressing salon for ladies was upstairs, but the reception desk was downstairs; it was a rather long, glass fronted counter. There was also a barber shop behind the glass partition. Mr. Peters rented it to David Ford who ran a one-man business. David was a bit of a rascal who liked the ladies. He was married to his first wife. It was one of my duties, to take the money off the clients and make new appointments; both the till and the appointment books were downstairs. If ever David wasn't busy and had no customers in his salon; he would pounce out on me and chase me around the counter; although I was intrigued, I made sure, he never caught me (a) because he was married (b) he was ten years older than I was and more importantly, I was in love with my husband and wouldn't dream of cheating on him

After working there for about a year, Mr Peters decided to retire from the business and sold it to (Arthurs the barber shop across the road). Mr Peters, not being an organised or honest man neglected to put my apprenticeship in writing; so the new owners were not obliged to employ me, they only wanted fully trained staff; so it meant I was out of a job once more. David also fared badly, as Mr Peters neglected to sign the lease on his salon and the new owners were not about to rent the salon to competition; he also had to find other premises.

After I left the hairdressers, I went to work in Wellworthy's where Terry worked. It was in a different section, which was why it was possible for him to make a fool of me so easily. The department I worked in was inspection. There was a dividing wall between us and the rest of the factory, so you could not see what the rest were getting up to. The name of the manager of our department was Mr Ball. I can only liken him to Charles Dickens' character (Mr Squeers). If you needed to go to the lavatory, you had to put your hand up and ask permission just like being at school. If you put a sweet in your mouth and he spotted you, he confiscated them. His wife also worked with us and although she was just an ordinary worker like us, she behaved, as though she was also the boss. After two years of that, I found myself another job. I went back into work and took great delight in telling Mr Ball what to do with his job.

My new job was in a cinema working behind the confectionery counter. The cinema was called the Odeon it is now the City Hall. I also had to sell ice-cream during the interval. On hindsight, that was a bad move because it meant I had to work every afternoon and evening, giving Terry plenty of scope for mischief. I wish I knew then what I know now. I could have saved myself years of heartache.

While I was working in the cinema, my friend Ann had her first baby, Susan she was a lovely baby; she was born, on the 30 January 1957. At first every thing seemed well, but suddenly she went into post natal depression and was ill for a long time. I used to see her on my days off when I used to accompany Harry; he was very distressed about it. Gradually, she got well again Susan was about seven months old before she was well enough to go home. She had another little girl on the 14 of July 1961, that was Linda and thankfully there were no problems.

When Susan was about two years old, Ann and Harry bought a plot of land and built a lovely bungalow. It took them about a year to build, mostly, by themselves; Harry was a carpenter by trade, but he would turn his hand to anything and with the help of a few friends in other trades, they built a lovely home.

I remember the house warming party, it was hilarious. My eldest daughter Carol was about two, Susan a year older and Jacqueline my second daughter, was a tiny baby. We put the children to bed before the other guests arrived, Susan in her own bed and my two, in Ann and Harry's bed. When the guests arrived they all put their coats in the main bedroom on the bed, without looking to see if there was anyone in the bed.

A great evening was had by all and all the men had too much to drink. Every now and again one or two of the men would disappear into the garden; we assumed they had gone out to be sick. We were not wrong, but unfortunately, Ann used to keep her vegetables, in a large holdall by the back door, it seems, they all used this and in the morning, she found this bag full of sick and had to throw the whole lot away.

My husband myself, and two babies, were invited to stay the night. They had a bed-settee in the sitting room, so I decided to give my baby her last feed, but when I went to the bedroom to find her, I couldn't see her. She had been buried under a pile of coats. I panicked and thought they had been suffocated, but they slept peacefully through it all.

All through the children's growing up, Ann and I became very close. We took it in turn to visit each other one week to her and one week to me. She was always there for me when I needed her and I'd like to think I was always there for her. That's what friends are all about.

I called upon her friendship many times over the years. I don't know what I would have done without her, if she hadn't been there for me.

When Jacqui was about ten months old, Terry informed me, we were going to move to Southampton to live; he said there was more work there. We sold our caravan and used the money as a down payment on a very classy, larger caravan with separate bedrooms, bathroom, kitchen and a large lounge with a verandah. It was all electric with an outside loo; I was happy to go because we needed more space and we were getting away from his mother.

He was working in partnership with his friend Roy Tredwell. The caravan was sited, in a caravan park in Allington Lane, West End. It had a little shop but everything was so expensive. If I needed to go to the village I had to walk a couple of miles with two babies in the pram.

He really put himself out for me at first. He bought us a T.V. set and a washing machine to make life easier for me or so I thought. but he was soon back to his old ways staying out till all hours and not paying for the things he bought on hire purchase. Pretty soon we were in a worse state than before. Everything was repossessed including the caravan and now we were homeless. I was by now six months pregnant with my third daughter, so I had to write to my mother and ask her if she would put us up until we got another place to live. There was no other choice and it turned out to be quite a nightmare. My mother was not into housework, the place was filthy and it took me weeks to clean the place fit enough for my children.

We bought two, three foot beds and put them together and all four of us had to sleep together. My mother had no intention of changing her ways, so I had to do all the cooking and cleaning, as far as she was concerned, she went to work all day and she was not going to do any housework; I don't think she even washed a cup.

We had put our names down on the housing list as soon as we were married and as we were desperate for somewhere to live. We started pestering the council on a weekly basis. We had been on the list for almost eight years and in the end they told us that if we did not stop bothering them, they would take us off the list altogether.

Patricia was born on the eighteenth of June 1961. We squeezed a cot into our already crowded bedroom and my mother would not allow the baby to cry at night. If she cried, she would march into the bedroom and order me to pick her up and feed her to shut her up. We pestered the council again and this time we got a house on the grounds of over crowding. We moved into our brand new, three-bedroom house at 42 Hoadley Green in March 1962 and it seemed like heaven. Of course we had the problem of furnishing it. We already had the children's beds and the baby's cot, but we managed.

That Easter we decided to tackle the garden. It was like a building site, which of course, is what it was, being a new house. We went to the Co-Op hardware shop to buy a fork and hedge trimmers. Terry did all the talking and asked the man behind the counter for the things we wanted. The man brought normal man-sized tools and asked Terry to get the feel of it for comfortable handling, to which he replied "Don't give it to me, give it to her. I don't keep a dog, and bark myself." The man was very embarrassed and took the tools back and returned with lady-sized tools. That weekend while we were working in the garden there was a knock on the front door, when we answered there were two young American lads, about eighteen or nineteen; they had come to preach the word of God and we assumed that they were exchange priests from the local church, so we invited them in. It turned out they were Mormons. They came in on my husband's invitation they asked if they could come again and we said yes. They started coming regularly and we met some of their elders; they were charming people. My husband found out that in the early years the Mormons had practiced polygamy, so he decided we must be having sexual orgies. So every time he saw them in the street wheeling their bicycles, he would say, "Here come, your boyfriends." He made my life a misery, so in the end I had to ask them not to come any more.

Life became steadily worse, both financially and emotionally. He decided to be self employed. He had no idea how to run a business. He employed two men to whom he paid more money than he paid himself. He just liked the idea of playing the big boss. The only people to suffer were his family; we had to make do with little or no money.

The winter of 1962-63 was horrendous. It snowed and it lay deep for three months. There was no work to be had; every thing was buried in snow. Carol started school in the January and picked up every child ailment going, measles, mumps, chickenpox, and scarlet fever. You name it, she caught it. The problem was that each of the other children caught it in turn. We were house bound for about twelve weeks. The youngest, Tricia, caught measles and chicken pox at the same time and was very poorly indeed. There were complications with the result being that one of her eyes turned up and outwards I took her to the doctor and before I could say anything, he spotted what was wrong and told me what I had come to see him about. The doctor sent her to Odstock hospital to see the eye specialist, who prescribed glasses to correct the problem. She was only eighteen months old and it was an absolute nightmare trying to keep those glasses on her. She would pull them off and frequently break them in half. It was a full time job going to the opticians to have them repaired.

After Tricia was born, the doctor advised me to go on the contraceptive pill with the result that I put on a tremendous amount of weight. I went from nine stone to about eleven. After two years of this the doctor said he was taking me off the pill for six months to give my body a rest, and then we could try something different. Well, I lost the weight, but I also got pregnant and had another miscarriage.

During that bad winter, having no work things became desperate and because Terry was self-employed, we were not entitled to any unemployment benefits. Give him his due, he was prepared to do anything, except work for any one else. So he used to drive cars for someone to and from different places and get paid for each car he delivered. Once he had to deliver a car to Shaftesbury and there was no way for him to get back except to walk. It was a freezing, snowy night and he had to walk from Shaftesbury to Bishopdown. It took him all night and he came home tired and cold and I felt very sorry for him. Then he did something really stupid. He got mixed up with some people who were stealing tyres and selling them on. Needless to say he got caught and the next day we were visited by the police. I was mortified and embarrassed, as if we didn't have enough problems. I can't remember exactly what happened next but he had to declare himself bankrupt. The receivers came and took away everything except the beds and the cooker and we had to buy back anything we needed on hire purchase.

Terry started staying out till the small hours and I could not go to bed till I knew he was home for the night; I also kept finding condoms all over the place; in the top pocket of his jacket, at the top of his wardrobe in the glove compartment of the car. His explanation was, he was looking after them for a friend. He must have thought I was really stupid.

From that day on he made sure the car door was kept locked; In fact, I was never allowed in the car except when we had to visit his mother. He hated to be proved wrong in anything or to be found out. His only answer was to lash out with his fists. I never learned, but I refused to roll over and die just to please him. I could only see right and wrong I did not allow for any grey areas in my life.

About that time I decided I would like to learn how to drive. So I sent away for my provisional licence. When it arrived Terry asked me; "why, where do you think you're going, if you do learn?" I just want to learn I said. It was the middle of winter and he said alright, I'll teach you. He took me out in the middle of a snow storm on the most dangerous road he could find, the main Salisbury to Amesbury road for my first lesson. It was the scariest thing I had ever done. All the while, he criticised and shouted at me. By this time I was a bundle of nerves, so when we reached the High Post Hotel, I stopped the car got out and told him to drive the damn thing himself. He obviously got the desired result. When the summer arrived, I sent for my licence once more hoping to have another try. When I told him, he said, "Don't waste your money, because your not driving my bloody car" so that was the end of that.

After a while, I was so fed up with his behaviour that if he wasn't back by midnight, I used to put the catch down on the front door so he could not let himself in, not even with a key. He would roll in about two or three in the morning, find he could not get in and started throwing stones up at my window I refused to answer, knowing I would be punished in the morning. He had to spend the night in the car, whatever the weather.

He was a lousy husband and an even worse father. He never had any time for his children. We used to have a large cardboard box that we kept behind the settee for the children's toys. They were very good about putting their toys away before they went to bed. But he could not bear to see their toys about. He would walk in, stand at the door and say, "Bang! It looks as though a bomb, has hit the place." I'd say they always put them away when they have finished with them, so where's the harm? He said, "I want them in bed before I get home." He would not let me or his children ever sit on his knee, yet other people's children were no problem; that really used to make me angry, to see him push his children away.

Because he earned the money, he thought he could spend it as he wished; he drank, he smoked and he always had to have a car, which he changed every two years, whether he had finished paying for the one he had already. I always kept an accounts book. I could tell you to the penny what I was given and what I had spent. He used to give me the housekeeping on a Friday and every day he would ask me for petrol money, cigarette money, or anything else he needed it for. Towards the end of the week, when I didn't have any more to give him, he would say, what have you done with all the money? I would show him the book, but he wasn't interested. So I told him to do the housekeeping himself. So he did for about three weeks and then asked me to take over again. I found out that he hadn't paid any bills or rent and we were in a bigger mess than before. Every time the rent man called, the children and I had to hide in the cupboard under the stairs, so he would not, find us in. It took quite a while to catch up with the back rent.

Life went on like this; until I was so fed up I told him I was leaving. I told him he could have the responsibility for a change. I packed my bag and walked out, leaving the children with him. I had no idea where I was going, I had nowhere to go. It was about eight o'clock in the morning. I caught the bus into town and left my suitcase at the bus station and wandered around in a daze till the left luggage office closed. I picked up my case and went home because I wondered if the children were fed or what was happening to them. I walked in to find three hungry children sitting at the kitchen table and my husband frying, or rather burning, sausages for them. All he did when I walked in was laugh and said, "I knew you'd be back."

I did a great many jobs to try and augment our finances, private hairdressing, sewing, dress making, even out-work for the firework factory. They delivered three sacks of tubes, labels, touch papers and glue. I used to have to stick the labels and touch papers to the tube and when they dried, twist the touch papers and stack them in bundles of twelve or thirteen, put rubber bands on them and pack them in boxes; all, for four old pence, a bundle. The whole family helped, including my husband and if we worked really hard we could earn three pounds a week. The poor children were sick of twisting touch papers, but it was a necessary evil.

In 1963, my sister Janet's husband, Brian, was posted to Cyprus. She wanted to go with him, but I believe she had to pay her own fare, so she asked me if I would look after her small daughter Debbie, so she could get a job and save up and join him. She paid me one pound, ten shillings per week, so it was a help to us both. My other sister, Geraldine was a single mother; she had a baby daughter called Gaynor. My mother decided that I should look after her baby also. She was quite a good baby actually, but she grew to be a very nasty adult, but that was down to her upbringing.

On several occasions they brought the baby over on Sunday saying my sister had to work. I later found out it was a lie and that she just wanted to be rid of the baby, so my sister could go out and enjoy herself. I was furious and told her I would not baby sit anymore to which my mother replied, "What difference does it make, you have so many children, one more won't hurt."

Geraldine met and married a divorcee by the name of Ronnie Bray. She was already pregnant with his son, Matthew and thankfully she went to live in his home in Yorkshire. After about a year or so later, he threw her out and she returned to Salisbury. Nine months later she gave birth to her third child, Rachael. I awoke to the sound of pebbles on my bedroom window. It was three o'clock in the morning. I looked out of the window and saw mother standing there. "Geraldine is in labour," she said, "come and phone the ambulance. I don't know how to use the public phone." I got to the phone and arranged for them to come. Then mother said you'd better come and clean up, I don't want the ambulance men to see the mess. When I got to the house, my sister yelled at my mother saying, "What did you bring her for?" "To clean up your mess," I replied. "You are worse than a farm yard animal. They only have sex for the purpose of procreation; you just follow your urges." (Her words, not mine.) My mother turned to me and said, "What about yours, they all have different fathers one's the baker's, one's the milkman's, one's the butcher's." To which I replied, "If I had one by the baker I would be in the Guinness Book of Records; my baker, is a woman! Unlike her all my children have the same father." To which mother said, "At least she is human, unlike you."

When Rachael was about two years old, Terry took to visiting my mother's house while she was at work during the day; I thought it rather odd, so I asked why. "I'm just going to borrow some books," he replied. I have never seen him read anything bigger than a comic book and he used to be gone for about an hour. I became suspicious and followed him one day. The back door was unlocked and I walked in. There was a scuffling sound and my sister came down stairs, in nothing but a dressing gown. "Where's Terry?" I asked, "In the bathroom." she replied. I knocked on the door and asked, "What are you doing in there?" "Reading," he said. "Why can't you read in your own bathroom?" No answer. "I'll be out in a minute," he said. A few days later I followed him again. This time they made sure that both the back door and the front door were locked. I knocked on the door, but nobody answered. I tackled them both about it, but they said it was all my imagination and there was no one in and Terry said he didn't even go there. I could not prove anything, so I let it drop until my mother hinted that Rachael was the spitting image of one of my daughters. They could be sisters, she said. I have never been able to prove it one way or another but unfortunately with my mother, you never knew when she was just being spiteful.

Mum was expert at humiliating me; on one occasion she had news that her sister was going to visit. She was over from Canada on holiday; she asked me if I would come and clean the house for her in readiness for her visitors; so I obliged and then she told me she didn't think there would be enough meat to go round, she said if I was going to eat there, I should provide one of the chickens; so I went to the shop and bought a large chicken and she added it to the pilau she was making. She invited lots of people, my brother and family, my sister and family, cousins and friends; I and my children were there entertaining the visitors and when lunch was ready she said to me in front of everybody; you can go home now and feed your children, there's not enough for you; I was speechless and my brother said, "don't go, you can have half of mine I said "no thank you;" I then left, so as not to cause any more embarrassment. My children had to have fish fingers because I had spent my money on her chicken.

After Janet and Brian were posted back home, they were posted to an air force camp in Cambridge; they had a son while in Cyprus. After a while she suspected he was up to no good; he liked young girls, very young and when his daughter was about fourteen, he left my sister for a sixteen year old girl, whom he eventually married. The divorce was held in Southampton, and I drove her there and back. After her divorce, Terry and I took her with us to which ever event we went to; so she did not get left out; even after I got divorced myself I included her in all my firms, outings. At one of my firms Christmas dances, she asked if I could get another ticket, as she had met someone; well I obliged and she arrived with Robert; I recognised him but could not place him. "I know you don't I," I said, "I don't think so", he replied. "Did you live in Wilton I asked"; "no he said" I then said," I never forget a face and when I remember who you are, I'll let you know". When I remembered, I felt sick; I just proved him a liar; he did live in Wilton, not far from me. He was living with a most undesirable family; one of the daughters had a baby by him.

My sister informed me she was going to marry him "no don't" I said, "live with him if you must; but don't marry him he is scum;" to which my sister replied, "it's too late we are buying a house together"; to add insult to injury, she asked me to make her wedding outfit; I grudgingly agreed.

The marriage did not last long; almost three years to the day and then he left to go back to his first wife. They came back while my sister was at work and stripped the house of everything valuable and also cashed the endowment policy and the house was repossessed because she could not pay the mortgage on her own.

7

My mother-in-law used to visit once a week. She would be dropped off by her husband Jock, about two in the afternoon and stay till nine in the evening, when my husband would drive her home. Because she was unable to move very far, I waited on her hand and foot bringing her tea on a tray, trying to make her as comfortable as possible. In the winter when it was cold, I would offer her the chair nearest the fire, which she would always refuse saying it was too hot. Nothing I ever did was right in her eyes. When it was time for her to go home, she would say thank you for the tea but on the way home, she would complain about me. She said I was a sergeant major, with the children, that I was selfish, that I had left her in the coldest part of the room and hogged the fire and she had been freezing all day. He would then come home and have a terrible row with me for treating his mother that way. He would always take her word against mine.

Terry's sister got married the previous year in St. John's Church in Lower Bemerton. It was a lovely wedding and my two eldest girls were bridesmaids. They wore white with lemon sashes and we bought another dress to match, for the youngest girl and they looked really sweet, all of them. I bought myself a dress in tangerine. I felt and looked very smart. Terry's best friend, Eric Stokes, made the mistake of remarking how nice I looked. So now according to my husband, there was something going on between his best friend and myself; anyway, he got very drunk and that's the night he made me pregnant with my son.

My doctor was furious that I was pregnant again. He said that men like my husband should have weights tied to their fronts and added to each month so they would know how it feels. My three girls were born in

Odstock Hospital. I was worried about the welfare of the girls if I had to go to hospital to have the next one, so I asked my doctor if I could have a home birth. He said I could on the understanding that if he decided at the last minute that it wasn't safe, I would go to hospital; I agreed and started making plans for a home birth.

My son, John, who was due at the end of April, arrived more than two weeks late, at seven o'clock in the morning on Friday the eighth of May. He was very distressed and the midwife began to panic. She could not get the baby to cry. She thought he was still born. My husband was shouting "It's a boy, it's a boy!" I heard her smacking the baby and getting no response, but I was too far gone with the gas and air to realise there was anything wrong. She then cleared the mucus from his throat and there was a gurgling sound as he let out a yell. The look on the midwife's face, said it all. She later confessed to me that if the baby had been one day later, he would have been dead as the placenta had gone green from lack of oxygen. She also told me this birth was like an army exercise, she didn't have to hunt for anything, everything, was where I said it would be and everything was in its place, one of the easiest she had been to, except for the scare at the end. The novelty of having a son, didn't last long; for my husband. The doctor put me on the pill again and suggested that my husband have a vasectomy but Terry would not hear of it so I had to go on the pill again and he carried on with his social life, which did not include me

My son was a good baby, no trouble at all sleeping all day and all night. In fact I had to wake him up for his feeds. Sometimes I would wake him just to make sure he was still breathing. When he was old enough to have his triple vaccinations I took him along to the local child clinic. The lady doctor looked to be way past retirement age and it worried me to see her straining her eyes to read the label on the phial. In fact she held the phial right up to her glasses to read it. About a week after his injection, he became very ill. The doctor said it was Whooping Cough, he was poorly for three months and after that until he was fourteen, he was susceptible to every respiratory ailment.

Because he was so small and so ill, he took up a lot of my time, which didn't help Tricia who was extremely jealous of her brother. Worst of all, I got no sleep for about six weeks and by then the insides of my eyelids felt like grit. Terry refused to take a turn in seeing to the baby at night. He said he had to go to work in the morning and you have all day to sleep. In fact, he was like that with all his children. If any of them were unwell, he would say, "You can sleep downstairs with them. You are not disturbing my sleep."

Just before my son was born, we had our tenth wedding anniversary. As usual, he never bothered and as usual I bought him a present and a card. He accepted my present, which was a shirt as I recall. He took the card unopened, over to the waste paper basket and dropped it in saying, "I don't believe in this rubbish. I'm trying to forget it." You have no idea how much that hurt.

Christmas 1964, we invited my brother and his family to spend Christmas with us. They had three children and we had four. The baby slept in our room, the other children doubled up in their beds and my brother and his wife were downstairs on the bed-settee. On Christmas Eve my brother said to me "What has Terry bought you for Christmas?" "The usual," I replied. "And what might that be?" he asked. "Nothing," I said, "I've not had a card or a present for Christmas, birthday or anniversary since the third anniversary." Denzil said, "We are going to show him up; I'm going to buy you a present and send it from him and see how he reacts. What would you like?" He bought me a pretty black nightdress, wrapped it and put it under the tree. Next morning, when all the presents were open I looked for the surprise on Terry's face but there was none; it was totally expressionless. I thanked him hoping he would feel bad but he kept up the pretence. I said nothing until the following anniversary when as usual he didn't bother. So I asked him, how he can accept my gifts, yet get nothing for me. To which he replied, "I bought you a nightdress for Christmas, what more do you want?" "You didn't even do that," I said and let him know what had occurred. He wasn't in the slightest bit embarrassed.

He was a very uneducated person. I had to write all his letters and he would copy them in his own handwriting to make out he had written them himself. I bought him a small dictionary to encourage him to be independent and to be able to answer the children if they asked him any questions. I wanted them to look up to him, but he wasn't interested. If the children asked him anything he would say, "Go and ask your bloody mother." In all the years that the children went to school, he only went to the parents' open day once. He just didn't want to know.

On the few occasions that we took the children out for the day, he would take the car for a wash, fill up with petrol, come home and expect me to have them all ready, including a packed lunch. If I wasn't ready, he would shout. If I asked "why can't you help with the children"? He would say, "It's not my job. "I've washed the car and put the petrol in, that's my job". Wherever we went, we always got lost and according to him it was always my fault and we'd end up arguing. He ruined every outing like that. The only time we had an outing where we didn't row, was when we had to take his mother with us, which was more often than not. Then she would dictate where and when we would go because of her disability. My mother would then get jealous and want to come also, so we very rarely got away by ourselves.

My mother lived only a few streets away, she worked as a nurse in the local hospital; when she finished work, instead of going home, she would come to our house and settled in for the evening; she expected to be fed and dictated what programmes we should watch on the television for the evening; if we wanted to watch something else, she would chat loudly until Terry got mad and slammed out of the house in a temper; then she would say, oh good now we can turn over and she would not go home till midnight and that was excuse enough for Terry to stay out late.

By the time John was four I was almost tearing my hair out. I didn't have a life, I was having to, live, by everybody else's rules and to make matters worse, Terry's stepfather was becoming a bit too familiar. I did not know how to cope with it so I told Terry to have a word and put a stop to it. Instead, he said I must have encouraged it. In the end, being at the end of my tether, the next time he made advances I shouted at him, "What makes you think I would look at an old goat like you?" He was taken aback, but it did the trick and he kept his distance after that.

I decided I would like to move away from Bishopdown and away from my mother. Also we needed something a bit bigger with a growing family. We arranged to do an exchange with a family, in Wilton. They neglected to tell me they were running away from the family, next door. If I had known then what I was getting into, we never would have moved. But that's another chapter.

We moved to Ditchampton, in March 1969. It was snowing and very cold. I had already arranged for the children to go to the local school except for John, as he was not yet five. The children soon settled. There was a riding stables nearby and my children were mad keen to ride, I allowed them to go every other week, as I could not afford to let them go every week. The people who lived to one side of us were some of the nicest people you could ever meet, Mr and Mrs Angove and their son Glyn. On the other side were the neighbours from hell. As far as the mother was concerned, the boys could do as could do as they wished. They blocked up my outside drains with bricks and banana skins, sawed through my down pipes, so when it rained, water would spurt out everywhere. When we had a wooden fence erected, they sawed through that. They used to light bonfires under my washing. They would torment the dog. They would stand at their back bedroom window with an air gun and shoot at our pets; I was always finding pellets in the rabbit hutch, I don't know how they missed him. I called the police out at least once a week, but the family would deny even owning a rifle. They used to take it to their grandmother's house, down the road and hide it.

This battle raged on for years. I complained to the council, but they refused to do anything about it. All they said to me was they would never move them as they would lower the tone wherever they went and that they would rather leave them where they were and move us to a new house if we wished. I retorted that if you had one bad apple in a barrel of apples, are you going to throw out all the good ones? They said, in this case yes, because they cause trouble wherever they go. They were building a new estate in a field along Burcome Lane and they offered us first choice if we would wait, so that's what we decided to do.

In the summer of 1969, we invited my sister Jan and her family to spend a couple of weeks with us. My brother-in-law was just as big a womaniser as my husband, only he liked them young, very young. During their stay, he and my husband used to go out by themselves quite a lot and unbeknown to us wives, they picked up a couple of girls in a pub. After the family went back home, Terry continued to see the girl he was with. I was still working in the evenings to make ends meet, but instead of staying in with the children, he would make the children go to bed almost as soon as my back was turned, threaten them with a beating if they got out of bed and sometimes beat them through the bed clothes so the bruises didn't show; then he would get dressed and go and see his girl friend. He would get back just in time to meet me when I got home from work. He made out he was taking the dog for a walk. This went on for many months and I knew nothing about it, the children never told me a thing, they were too scared; I only found out about it after the divorce, more than ten years later.

Christmas of 1969, we invited my sister and family to stay; both men decided to go out for a drink, while my sister and I prepared lunch. They were gone so long that we decided to have our lunch without them; when they finally arrived, I warmed the food and dished up. Terry only ever ate breast meat; he would never have anything with a bone in it. When I brought the food to the table, he decided Brian's dinner was bigger than his and he threw a tantrum, when I explained, the only thing different was Brian had a leg, apart from that, everything was the same; he picked up his plate and threw his dinner up the wall.

Our sex life disappeared and if I ever snuggled up to him in bed, he would swear at me and tell me to f--- off, get over to your own side of the bed he would say. If I persisted, he would slam out of the bedroom and sleep downstairs. Naturally I got upset, so he tried to pacify me by saying he was not well.

If he wanted to go out on his own with no questions asked he would create a row. He was expert at this. He could make a row out of nothing, so that he could storm out of the house in righteous indignation. I slowly cottoned on to his tricks and wouldn't play ball, so he had to think of something else. His next ploy was to say "there's a good film on TV, that he must see, tonight". After we settled down to watch, he would suddenly look at his watch and say, "I've just remembered, I have to see a man about a job he wants priced, won't be long." then I wouldn't see him again till the small hours of the morning.

He became a bit more cheerful for a while. He used to waltz me round the room singing, "Please release me let me go, cause I, don't love you, anymore." But he made such a joke of it, I wasn't a bit suspicious. Then came the time he told me he had to go away to work at the weekends. He would get me to scrub his back and pack his suit and pyjamas and clean underwear. He would load all his tools of the trade in his car and he'd be gone from Friday evening till Sunday night. What I did not know was that he was spending his weekends with this girl in Bulford Camp's married quarters. Her name was Louise Margaret May and she was about six years younger than I was and came from British Guyana. She was married to a British soldier, who was serving abroad at the time and she was playing away while he was away.

As the months wore on he became more abusive both physically and mentally I used to get so stressed, that I would borrow my eldest girl's bicycle and ride off for miles, to calm down. One day in a fit of temper, he punched me in the face. I had two black eyes and he knocked my teeth out. I was spitting blood and teeth all over the place. When I asked him why, he said I provoked him. When I asked what in his view, was provocation, he could not answer. Luckily they were dentures, but I had the embarrassing task of going to see the dental technician to have them repaired. As much as I hate liars, I could not tell him I had been beaten up by my husband. So I had to lie and told him I had fallen over the handle bars of my daughter's bike. I don't think he believed me, but he said nothing and had them ready the next day. I could not go to work for a couple of days till the swelling went down then, I plastered my face with make-up to try and hide the bruises.

We started getting strange letters and phone calls asking my husband to go and see someone about something legal. When I queried it he said it was something to do with a job that had gone wrong and he would dash off to see someone. He was always terrified, when I answered the phone. All this nonsense went on for months and then on the first of April 1970, All Fools Day, it must have been the Easter holidays for the children, because I remember they were home that day and I was preparing lunch, I heard him come in and the next thing I knew, he had put his arms around my waist from behind while I was at the sink and started fooling around. He said, "I have something to tell you. Will you forgive me?" Because he was playing the fool, I said, "Ah! That depends." I never dreamt of what was to come. He told me about this girl and that she was eight months pregnant and of course he put the blame on her, saying she tricked him into making her pregnant. Apparently, she told him she was on the pill. I was so shocked I fainted away at his feet. He didn't tell me that he was sorry for what he had done. What he said was that he would not have had me find out for the world, which says a lot about him.

Call me a masochist if you like, but I insisted that he take me to see her. I got my neighbour to baby sit and he drove me to Bulford Camp. We pulled up to the house and I noticed several little black faces with runny noses at the window. I was shocked and did not know what to expect. He knocked on the door and we were admitted by the mother of those children. It turned out that she was the sister of his girlfriend. He ran straight up the stairs to her bedroom and after what seemed like an eternity, he brought her down. I wanted to kill her with my bare hands, but when I saw her swollen stomach, I couldn't.

When we came face to face, Terry turned to me and said, "The floor's all yours, act out your little drama." Before I could say a word, she started shouting, she called me a whore; "what the hell do you mean by that"? I asked." Well it stands to reason, she said. You have three daughters and the eldest girl is thirteen and you have only been married six years. I know the son is his, but you had all your girls by different men". I was shocked "I don't know where you got your information from I said; but we have been married for sixteen years and all my children belong to my husband". "He told me she said; that none of the girls were his". I looked at him and he looked back expressionless and made no excuses. So I walked out. He followed and told me she was lying. I wanted to believe him, but I knew in my heart that it was he who was lying.

We got home but life was never going to be the same again. If I had any sense, I should have thrown him out there and then. Instead I chose to accept his version of things. That night I needed to be comforted and I allowed him to make love to me and although I begged him not to he deliberately made me pregnant again. It festered in my mind for about three weeks, I couldn't eat or sleep; I paced the floor at night. I tried to carry on as normal for the children's sake, but the pain, both mental and physical, was too much to bear and one lunch time while the children were at school, I found I had a splitting headache, so I decided to take a pain killer, I went to the medicine cabinet to get a couple of tablets and while I was there I thought, what the hell, I might as well take the lot and did. I don't remember much about the next few hours, except I was sat in an armchair. I kept hearing bells and I remember saying repeatedly "God forgive me." The next thing I knew, Terry was trying to make me stand up, but I was very limp. He kept saying "what have you done?" Then he called the ambulance.

I have no recollection about the time of day, but I do remember arguing with the ambulance man and telling them it was none of their business and to leave me alone, that I could die if I wished; his answer was, I'm afraid it is our business, but they were very kind and gentle.

I was taken to the intensive care unit in Salisbury Infirmary and had my stomach pumped out. It was the most unpleasant experience of my life and when they finished, they put me on a saline drip. The ward sister was furious with me. She said how dare you do such a thing and she put me in a bed between two beds with young men in them who had been in car accidents. Both were stark naked and were covered by plastic covered half hoops. One of them had had a tracheotomy. I was very embarrassed and I think this was what she intended.

After a couple of days, I was visited by a psychiatrist who said if I promised not to do anything silly again I could stay in hospital a few more days and then go home. The nursing sister was outraged, "she's not staying in my ward, she said, take her away". So they sent me to the Old Manor. When I realised they were going to send me to a mental hospital, I fought like a wild thing I refused to go there. The next thing I knew, I was sedated and bound to the stretcher and was sectioned for six weeks all because the nursing sister decided she did not like me. It's a pity she did not know, what I was going through.

I woke up three days later in Nightingale Ward. The other patients said, thank God for that. Apparently, I had been crying hysterically non-stop for the last three days but I was unaware of it. It was a very depressing place also a bit scary, because there were some people there with real mental problems.

I had an appointment with the resident psychiatrist. He said "there is nothing we can do, no drugs we can give you to make things better. Only you can decide, you either accept things as they are or divorce him." I said I would think about it, but in the mean time I said, "I'm pregnant. So what harm have I done, to the baby, by taking an overdose;"" how do you know you are pregnant" he asked;" I just know", I said. He had some tests done and agreed with me; he then sent me to see the gynaecologist.

When I saw the gynaecologist, I asked again," will the baby be deformed because of what I had done". He said "possibly", so I said I would like a termination rather than bring a disabled baby into the world because of something I had done. His reply shocked and upset me. He said, "are you sure it's not because the baby is not your husband's"? I was livid how dare he say such a thing, but for all I know Terry could have put the idea into his head.

Anyway I had the abortion on my birthday, the eighteenth of May 1970 The only person to come and visit me on my birthday was my friend Ann. She brought me a large bottle of perfume and we both cried and she told me how much she hated Terry.

My sister-in-law helped her brother round the house whenever she could, but she had two small children of her own, so obviously she could not be there all the time. So all the important things like laundry, wasn't being done regularly and when they started letting me go home at week-ends, I had to face huge piles of washing and ironing. It seems that's all I was doing on my home visits, as the children had run out of clean clothes. It got to the stage, where I did not want to go home.

On my first day after I was released, from the hospital, I was visited by my mother-in-law. She was dropped off by her husband.

As soon as he had gone, she turned on me. "Why have you got my son tied to your apron strings? He hates you, you know. The children hate you as well; they can't wait to be eighteen, so they can leave home. Terry told me that the reason you tried to commit suicide, was because you were in so much debt, you were taking the easy way out." This, after only a few hours out of hospital was a bit hard to take. He had neglected to tell her about the girl friend or the baby and when I enlightened her, she called me a liar. She struggled to her feet and left the room. She could not leave the house, so she sat on the stairs near the front door, so she would be the first one to see Terry when he came home from work. As soon as she heard the key in the lock, she started screaming, your wife this and your wife that. I came out of the sitting room and told him in front of her what she had said. He said to her "If you can't speak to my wife any better than that, don't bother to come again." I said "take her home now and I don't want to see her ever again." she shouted to him "Don't let her speak to you like that, our Terr." which is what she called him. "Hit her, go on hit her." Well I never saw her for about eight years after that. I never stopped him from seeing her and I never prevented the children from visiting either, but she still continued to try and wreck my marriage, by poisoning the children's minds.

One day after a visit to their grandmother, my middle daughter, Jacqueline, said "Do we have to go to see Nanny Jock?" as they called her. "Why?" I asked. "Well, she's always saying bad things about you. She says you are a bad mother and a bad wife and I just don't like it"; so I stopped the children's visits. I then started getting abusive phone calls from her husband because she was upset. "There are names for people like you," he would say. In the end, I just used to put the phone down on him; it saved a lot of unpleasantness. I knew it wasn't his fault; she just used to get him wound up till he had to do something. We never saw them again for a long time. Then just before Christmas 1978, for some unknown reason, I relented and invited them over for Christmas. I'm glad in a way; she was unusually pleasant and friendly. It must have been some sixth sense that made me make peace, because she died in the February of 1979.

I was told by the doctor that it was about time I came off the contraceptive pill as it was bad for me to be on it for as long as I had been. So I asked Terry if he would have a vasectomy so that I would not have the worry of becoming pregnant again. He refused, so I had to continue to take the pill. I had been asking him for about seven years without success, when suddenly he suggested it. I was surprised, but pleased. We went to see the doctor and he made arrangements for us to visit the surgeon at the hospital. This was about 1973 or 74. The surgeon made an appointment for the operation and told me to deliver my husband in the morning and to pick him up that evening when the anaesthetic had worn off. I called at five o'clock and they said he had not come round sufficiently to be allowed home.

Would I come back about seven? When I went to collect him at seven, I said "thank you darling, for doing this for me". He turned to me in front of a ward full of men and said, "Don't kid yourself I didn't do it for you, I did it so I can have a letter in my pocket saying I'm safe." there were no limits to his cruel tongue. It was a long time, before we had sex again; he didn't seem interested. He intimated that he had lost his manhood and that it was all my fault.

When he decided he wanted sex, he would wait till I was almost asleep, with my back to him, then he would start touching me in a sexual way; if I responded and turned towards him, he would say, "don't turn round, I don't want to have to look at your face;" I was offended by his rudeness and would tell him so, then he would say; "forget it I'll do it myself," and he would masturbate beside me.

In 1971, for the first time in our marriage, he decided to take us on holiday to Butlins where all the meals were included It was a good experience for the children as they had never had a holiday before. We went again in 1973, half board and again in 1975 self catering. In 1972, my neighbour, Mrs Angove, asked me if I was learning to drive. "No," I said, "why do you ask?" "Well!" she said, "I saw some L plates on your husband's car." "You must be mistaken," I said. She was not wrong, after a while, I noticed, the L plates myself. "Who are you teaching to drive?" I asked. "nobody." he said. "Then why have you got L plates on your car?" he had forgotten to take them of; "Oh! Just one of the lads down the road," he said. "If it's good enough for your friends, then it's good enough for me. I am going to send for my provisional licence and you can stick your car, I will get proper driving lessons." So he decided to take me out for lessons with him with the intension of putting me off. He would scream and shout and make me a nervous wreck. In the end I said, "forget it, I will get a proper instructor;" so I hired Andrew Baylis; he was thorough and patient and after three failures, he got me through.

To my great surprise, Terry bought me a second hand car; it was a dangerous car but I did not realise it till it broke down at the traffic lights; the gear change came off in my hand and I had to have it towed to the nearest garage, where they discovered the gear change was held in place with a spanner; so I began to wonder if he knew about it. It was welded back on and it was safe after that.

Carol's wedding, September 1982 from the left, John, Tricia, Carol, myself and Jacqui.

When my children were young, we had many pets, it was a veritable zoo. There was a dog, (a Dalmatian), an African Grey parrot, Budgerigars, Goldfish, Hamsters, a Dutch rabbit with one blue eye and one brown eye and a pair of gruesome looking Mexican newts called Axolotl. They looked like small black dragons with wavy branches growing out of their heads. I named them Grew and Some. To add to this, the children used to bring injured wild things home with them and expect me to make them well, which wasn't always possible. The only animal I would not allow was a cat. It was not that I would hurt one; it was just that I can't bear to be around them; I have no idea why, but they make the hair on my back stand on end.

It used to cost a fortune to feed them all, not to mention all the time it took to feed and clean up after them all. I know initially, they promised to exercise and clean and feed their pets, but inevitably it falls to mum or else the animals would starve and let's face it; as much as I fought against having the animals in the first place, I was totally hooked once they were installed. All except for the Axolotl which I used to have nightmares about, so when my second daughter Jacqui, became eighteen and moved into the nurses' home to do her training, I insisted she take them with her.

The dog we got as a puppy. He was all white apart from his ears, which had black tips and one black spot. Over the next few weeks we saw new spots forming until he looked like a proper Dalmatian. A more intelligent animal, you could not find. He seemed to know exactly what you were talking about. He was a brilliant guard dog and quite handsome. He was a pedigree, his kennel club name was Jason's Delight, but we called him Brutus. We did show him a few times, but he only ever came second; apparently, although he was quite beautiful, he was a bit too tall. He was a bit fussy about his food and if he did not like what you gave him, he would pick the bowl up in his jaws, take it out in the garden and turn it upside down. He would not drink water, not even if he were dying of thirst, until you coloured it with a drop of milk.

If we went out without him, we left him in the back garden in his kennel. He would take his frustration out on the lawn by digging a crater in the lawn. When we got back and I discovered the hole, I would take him to the hole and shout at him and tell him he was a naughty dog in my crossest voice. He would then put his head on the ground and put both front paws over his eyes. It was difficult to stay cross with him.

The African Grey parrot arrived by chance. He was perched in a tree in the back garden. He was only a young bird and was being attacked by other birds and next door's cats were after the parrot. So Jacqui climbed the tree and caught it; she almost had her thumb severed in the process, it had a lethal beak. We put it in a spare budgie cage and called the R.S.P.C.A. They arrived, took one look at the parrot and said, no thanks, you can keep it till we find the owners, but don't hold your breath, they probably turned it loose, to get rid of it. The children begged to be allowed to keep it, so we had to spend a fortune to get a proper cage. Transferring it from one cage to another was no mean feat. It got loose and caused havoc, destroying everything in sight using that beak. It made holes in my new curtains, I was none too pleased. After we put him in his new cage, I made sure he stayed there till he got used to the family. The trouble was he knew how to open the cage by himself, so I had to put a padlock on to keep him in. Once he settled down and realised no one wanted to harm him, he was given the freedom of the house and he made a wonderful pet. He was a gifted talker and had a wide repertoire. He would bark, meow, growl, sing and talk really well. He mimicked my voice particularly well and he would call out "Brutus!" in my cross voice and the poor dog, didn't know if he was coming or going. He would look up at me as if to say, what have I done now?

The rabbit was named Bugsy. He was black and white like the dog and I'm sure he thought he was a dog also. He had the freedom of the house and garden; we only ever locked him in his hutch at night. Bugsy and Brutus used to take it in turns to chase each other round the garden or sometimes you would find them asleep together in the dog basket. The rabbit was a charming creature and when he died at the age of eight, I was heart broken, I cried all day.

We had several hamsters and as they are short lived animals, usually about two years, you could guarantee when they died, I would be the only one to cry.

The budgerigars were very entertaining. We only had them one at a time; the first one flew away, the second drowned in the fish tank, (it went in after the weed) and the third one lived to a ripe old age. It was a hen bird, but she became a good talker. We just had to make sure we never let the budgie and the parrot out at the same time or the parrot would have attacked the budgie for sure.

We also had a tortoise which we should have called Houdini. He certainly was an escape artist and extremely fast for a tortoise; whenever we allowed him out of his enclosure, he would race to the top of the garden and climb over the wire fence, into the field and we would have to look for him. I no longer have animals as I now live in sheltered accommodation and pets are not allowed, they also need exercise, which at my age, am not able to give.

We moved to our new house, in Randall's Croft Road on the 15th of January 1975. It was a four bedroom end of terrace, with a small front garden and a slightly larger back garden. It was very up to the minute for the time, with central heating, something we never had before and very much appreciated. I thought after moving away from the neighbours from hell, we could live in peace, but it was not to be.

I asked my husband if he could trade my car in, for a less thirsty one because having to drive to work, I found it very expensive to run. One with a smaller engine, I said.

He came back with an even greedier car, a Rover 3500. I won't dispute it was a lovely car to drive, but it was costing me about twelve pounds a week in petrol. The truth was it made him look good behind the wheel. He borrowed it every weekend to go out by himself.

Things got worse between us; he would tell me he was going out with his friends and he needed to borrow my car. He would even name the friends. Then I would find out from his friends that they had no such arrangements. He hated being in the wrong, most of all he did not like being found out; so he would sulk and would not speak to me, for weeks on end; if he wanted to say anything to me, he used to address me through the children.

He was still staying out till the early hours and I would wait up for him. Part of me would be worrying about him being in an accident and the other part of me would be wishing that he did. When he did decide to come home, he would race up the stairs, to the bathroom, leaving the door open; I watched from the bottom of the stairs and see him washing down the front of his trousers with a flannel; he didn't care whose flannel he used; then I had to put all the flannels in the wash, to make sure nobody used them after him.

The only time we went out as a family, was on Sunday evening to the club, as long as I paid; most of the time, he never even sat with us; so even when we were out, I was still on my own.

After Christmas 1975 he could not get any work, so I asked him to get any kind of job just to tide us over. I had a part time job, but it wasn't enough to pay the bills. His reply was "if I can't be self employed, I will be unemployed" and he meant it. Finally, he got himself a job delivering papers for a wholesaler at four o'clock in the morning for about sixteen pounds a week. It barely covered the cost of his cigarettes. When he got home, he then went to bed for half the day. This went on for about thirteen weeks and we were getting deeper and deeper in debt. We couldn't even afford to feed the animals.

One evening I said "we have to talk". His reply was "I don't want to listen to your rubbish." I told him, as he wasn't going to work, I would have to do full time. The only trouble was he had to get rid of the dog. He was not a well animal and I wasn't prepared to leave him on his own all day. He kept saying "no". This went on for weeks. In the end I took the dog to the vets and asked him if he could re-home, him for me, as we could not afford to keep him any longer and that I needed to go to work to make ends meet. The vet said it would be kinder to have him put to sleep, as he was not a well dog. Well, I cried so hard, the vet made me leave by the back door, so as not to upset the people in the waiting room.

I had to start my full time job the following Monday, so I still had to go to my part time job on that evening too. When I got home from work Terry was out which was not unusual, so when the children had gone to bed, I had a bath and washed my hair and put it in rollers; I then sat down to watch T.V.

Terry rolled in just before midnight, the worse for drink and said to me, "Where's my dog?" "You know where he is," I said, "we discussed it often enough." With that, he pulled me up by my hair and said, "I loved that dog more than I ever loved you." then he threw me around like a rag doll punching me and when I landed on the floor, he started using me like a football. The next morning my eldest daughter treated me like I was a murderer.

His mother became very ill at the beginning of 1979. It was obvious she was coming to the end of her life, so her husband asked if I could lend him one of my single beds, so that he could move her into the sitting room and make her more comfortable. I had the spare beds, as my middle daughter had become a student nurse and had moved into the nurse's home and my youngest daughter had run away from home at the age of sixteen.

When Terry's step-father arrived to pick the bed up, Terry insisted that I provide the bed clothes as well. I said we don't have any spare bedclothes and besides, his mother had a lot more bed linen than I did. To which his step-father replied, "Yes, we have loads of sheets and things." Terry then lost his temper and ranted and raged at me and called me all the names under the sun. It was all down hill from then on. Things became a lot worse when his mother died; he started calling me names, every four letter word in the book. He would not let us sit near him at the crematorium; we were not allowed to sit with the family. He never spoke to me for months after that.

My life was a living hell for a while. Then one morning, I awoke and said to myself, "Is this all there is to life?" So I moved out of our bedroom and into my youngest daughter's bed and not once did he question why. Nor did he ever ask me to come back to his bed.

It was our twenty fifth wedding anniversary on the 20th of March. We didn't celebrate it. It was no surprise, as he very rarely remembered, either Christmas birthdays or anniversaries. I did receive a bouquet of yellow roses I had assumed it came from my eldest daughter Carol, she was very thoughtful like that. I thanked her and said they were lovely, but I was left in ignorance of who the sender was because there was no card attached. About a week later I received the bill from the florist for £12 a lot of money in those days I asked him if he had sent the flowers; he replied "Who the hell else will?" I said "In that case you can pay for them" and I gave him the bill.

It was his birthday on 21st July, and for the very first time since we met, I deliberately forgot his birthday. I thought, let's see how you feel. He made no comment, mind you; by this time, as far as he was concerned, I was invisible. So I asked him to leave. He said "No, it's my house I will go when I'm ready." After a couple of weeks, I packed all his belongings and put them outside the front door. He came in anyway, so I asked him again but he did not reply. It was time for bed and as I had to get up early for work, I retired. All of a sudden, one of the children woke me to say dad has taken your car keys out of your handbag and stolen your car. I jumped out of bed, put my dressing gown on and rushed out of the house just in time to see him reverse the car out of the garage. So before he could drive away, I stood in front of the car to prevent him from driving off. "Get out of the way," he said, "or I'll run you over." I stood my ground, but he eased the car forward till I fell. He only stopped when my legs disappeared under the bonnet. He reversed, I picked myself up and he drove away.

The next day, I went to see a solicitor and was advised to go to the Council about getting the house put in my name. They said they could only do it if I was divorced and if one of the children was still at school, otherwise the husband gets the house. As luck would have it, my son was only fifteen, so I thought I'd better not waste time. I did not want life to drag on the way it was forever. It took several weeks to get my car back which made it difficult for me to get to and from work. It meant catching the bus at some ungodly hour to Salisbury and another bus from Salisbury to West Harnham and the same in reverse to go home, which added another two hours to my day. Before that I had always been home in time for the children.

I had joined a ladies darts team about a year earlier and had to ask his permission to do so, because he was so controlling; because they were short of a player, he said yes. So I used to go out every Monday evening to wherever the team were playing. He would tag along with one purpose in mind. Whenever it was my turn, he would criticise me and tell me how stupid I was if I did not hit the right number.

He still had a key to the house and let himself in, whenever I was out and helped himself to whatever he wanted. The Council would not let me change the locks because we were not divorced. He removed all the insurance policies although it was I who paid for them. My solicitor found out that he had left them with his accountant. They gave me the man's address and told me to collect them. The man refused, saying it was emotional blackmail. I reported this to my solicitor and when they wrote to him, he soon released them.

He did his level best to make my life as difficult as possible. He even tried to cancel my car insurance. I had a visit from my insurance man. He asked if he might see my car insurance policy. I asked why and he told me my husband has cancelled it. "He can't do that," I said "I paid for it myself." "Well it all depends on the wording," he said, "if it says Mr. Blake and spouse, then I'm afraid he can. But if it reads Mr. Blake and Mrs. Patricia Blake, then there's nothing he can do about it." Luckily it was the later.

Then he started parking his car outside the house and staying there till the small hours. The children would get upset and ask me to let him in; I refused. He then went to my neighbour and asked him to keep an eye on me, to make sure no men came to the house. My neighbour, Dave was furious, "How dare you talk about your wife like that. Piss off!"

His next trick was to keep phoning me to ask if he could come back. I said no, to which he replied, "But it is my home. My name is on the rent card." "Ok," I said "just tell me one thing you ever did to make it a home, and you can come back." He could not think of a thing. "But I love you," he said. "Well, I don't even like you," I replied and put the phone down. He then went into a downward spiral. He started drinking heavily and people kept finding him unconscious on the floors of pubs. His friends would tell me how mean I was not to have him back. I said "I have been through this a million times and enough is enough."

I decided to see a solicitor so I could get a separation order. I had no intentions of getting a divorce, all I wanted was to get him out of my life, to get some breathing space and stop him harassing me. The solicitor told me that he would have to send my husband a copy. That's fine, I replied. Shortly afterwards I received my copy and I suppose so did he; anyway, he phoned to say he would be coming by to collect some papers of his that he needed, I put the things he needed in a carrier bag, ready for when he called. He arrived that evening and I handed him the bag. He took the bag from my hand, pushed the door open and closed it behind him. He had not realised that my two eldest daughters were in the sitting room, with one of their boyfriends. He put the bag down and beat me to a pulp; the silly thing was, I was more concerned about getting blood on my new wallpaper than I was about my face. I had spent my annual holiday and some of my holiday money decorating the hall and stairs. He did not think I was capable, so accused me of having some man doing it.

I would not give him the satisfaction of seeing me cry. So when he had exhausted himself, I said, "Have you finished?" He said "Yes." "Now do you know what I'm going to do?" I said, "Something I should have done years ago." "And what's that?" he asked. "I am going to call the police." I picked up the phone. "No you don't!" he said and snatched the phone from my hand, ripped it out from the wall, threw it on the floor and jumped on it. "Now try phoning." he said. In the mean time, my girls and the boy friend had stayed in the sitting room, petrified. I called out to my daughter Jacqui, "Would you go down to the public phone box and call the police for me please?" "Yes mum." she replied. As she stepped out of the room, he snarled at her, in a threatening voice, "Don't you dare;" "Just you watch me," she said, and left. He ran off, before the police arrived. I had kept my tears in check because I wasn't going to let my husband see me cry, but when the police arrived and I had to speak, the tears flowed. The police checked my injuries and told me to see the doctor the following day to have my injuries recorded. They also advised me to see my solicitor and ask for a divorce. The separation order was not worth the paper it was written on, they said. The incident would be classed as a domestic and he could come and do this whenever he wanted. I was rather taken aback when my eldest daughter turned to me and said, "Did you cry because Dad hurt you or did you just cry for the police?" I was really hurt by this remark, but I let it go over my head. Anyway, I took their advice and was granted a divorce within six months.

Jacqui was engaged to a boy called **Richard**, for quite some time. Suddenly it was off, I never really knew why and it was none of my business. I rather liked him but you can't choose for your children. Before long she met her husband Keith, I think it was a rebound thing. They were married within weeks of meeting. I never cared for him at all. They arranged the wedding and told me about it about two weeks before the wedding. They were married on the 8th of December 1979 about five weeks before my divorce became absolute. She was adamant her father was not to attend the wedding, but I managed to persuade her. Whatever he had done to me, he was still her father. But she would not let him give her away, so I had to stand in for him. He was not happy about that and he got very drunk.

Shortly after my divorce in January 1980, while I was out playing darts with the ladies from the Wilton Club my eldest daughter got a phone call from the woman who had my husband's illegitimate daughter. When I returned home, I found my daughter sobbing her heart out. I asked her what was wrong. She yelled at me saying, "I am twenty one years old and you treat me like a baby." "What are you talking about?" I asked. "A woman phoned to ask if she could speak to Dad" she said, "I told her he no longer lives here. She then asked if I could give her his address and telephone number." My daughter asked who she was, and the woman said "Who are you?" my daughter replied, "I'm his daughter". The woman then asked, "How old are you," "twenty one," my daughter replied. "You're old enough," she said and told my daughter of her affair and that she had a half sister. She said she wanted to get in touch as she had got married and wanted her new husband to adopt her daughter and needed the father's permission. "Why didn't you tell me?" my daughter wailed. "Because what he did, he did to me, not you. If I wanted to poison your minds against him I would have done it years ago."

Carol married Stephen in September 1982, they married in St Mary and St Nicholas, in Wilton and I had the great pleasure of making all the wedding clothes, including my own outfit.

In the autumn of 1979 I was asked out by a man whom I worked with. His name was Fred and at first I turned him down. I said I was married and so are you. "You are not happy," he said, "or you would not be coming to work with black eyes and bruises. No man who is a man would ever hit a woman." I still said no but he was very persistent and after a few weeks, I thought why the hell not. Although I was not yet divorced from my husband, we were not living together. Also it was nice to feel desirable again. After that we met whenever we could, I did not even feel guilty about his wife; I had fallen in love. Our affair lasted till December 1982, when I discovered he was as big a cheat as my husband. He wasn't only cheating on his wife, he was also cheating on me; I was very upset, so it ended. I asked him for my front door key back, and I never saw him again.

I was made redundant from work, in the November of 1982 and was paid up till Christmas. We were told we were told we could not claim unemployment benefit till January 1983. I spent two months looking for work; writing in reply to every advertisement. The few that replied, told me I was too old, most didn't have the courtesy to reply at all. After the first of January I applied at the unemployment office and explained that I had been looking for work without success; I was shocked to find I was treated like a criminal. The office was filled with teenagers who had never worked and had no intention of working. I knew most of them personally, so I knew they were work shy. They were greeted like old friends, while I was treated like a fraud. Eventually they agreed to give two weeks money and advised, to make sure that if I managed to find a job, I was to tell them straight away, so they could stop my money. As luck would have it, I managed to get a job with Pains Wessex, to start the following week, on the understanding; we worked a week in hand. As requested, I informed the unemployment office, and told them my starting date; I received a very uncivil reply, demanding the return of the two weeks money. I went back to the office and asked them, what I am supposed to live on, till I get paid in two weeks time. After some consultation, they said, in that case you can keep it. As you can imagine, I was furious at being treated like that, especially after all the years of paying health insurance and tax, all my working life. Any way I started work at Pains Wessex, on the 17 of January 1983 and worked there till my retirement.

In the months following the divorce, I bumped into several women who said they had had an affair with Terry. Women that I had known as friends, one of them was Kathy whom I had been to school with. When I expressed my surprise and disappointment, she said "Oh well! It's all water under the bridge. Then there was Helen, the one he'd asked out years before. I'm glad you divorced him, she said, he was always no good. Joan was another school friend who told me he had picked her up from work and instead of taking her home, he took her out into the country and tried to rape her. He was supposed to be a friend of her boyfriend, Roy.

I never trusted any man after that. If any man tried to become too familiar, I sent him packing. That is how hurt I was. I still saw Terry on and off in connection with the children at weddings, christenings and such. I always made sure he had an invite to family gatherings; I can't think why. I can only suppose after twenty six years of marriage, there were still some feelings left. He often tried to manipulate meetings though the children by inviting them out and saying your mother is included, but very wisely I avoided the trap. He decided to buy his council flat, something he refused to do when we were married. When I asked him if we could buy our house, he replied, "I'm not having a mill stone round my neck for you." So I was rather annoyed that he could do it for himself. I was further annoyed when my sister Janet played hostess when he had a house warming party. I felt she was being disloyal to me. After all she knew how he had treated me all our married life. She kept it a secret. When I found out about it, I asked her why. "There was nothing sexual," she replied. "It's not about him," I said, "it's about you and me. Sisters don't do that sort of thing." She then said that she did not know that Terry used to beat me up; "you are a liar" I said you have always known; why else would you tell me that Brian only did it once and you told him, if he ever did it again, you would kill him, even if you had to wait until he fell asleep".

There were many women, in Terry's life. He changed them as often as he changed his socks. There was a Jean, a Shirley and God knows how many others after the divorce. Then he met Pauline and I knew instinctively that she was bad news. She loved only herself. It was quite laughable really, because no two people deserved each other more. She thought he had money and he thought she had money and they were both disappointed.

For a short time, for the first time in his life, he actually wanted to spend time with his children, and he spent money on them. This did not go down well with Pauline. She went to visit my eldest daughter and told her that her father was not to spend his money on them, as his money was now hers. She also slandered my name, saying she could name at least four men that their mother had slept with. My daughter came to see me to find out if it was true. I was outraged to think my daughter would even believe such a thing, so outraged that I went to the shop that Pauline owned and demanded that she name them. She had a shop full of people at the time and I wanted witnesses. "Name them," I said "and I'll have you in court." she started to cry saying Terry told her. One of her sons came towards me. "Get out of my mother's shop." he said. "When I have said, what I've come to say," I replied. He stretched out his hand towards me. I'm not sure of his intentions but I told him, "You put one finger on me son, and I'll break it off. Now I'll leave."

Obviously she must have phoned Terry, because when I reached home, he phoned. "Why did you embarrass Pauline in front of all her customers? Could you not have phoned her?" "Only cowards hide behind phones," I replied. "Anyway, how dare you tell lies about me?" "I didn't," he said, "she made that up." "Well I haven't finished yet," I said, "I will see my solicitor and see what she says." What she said was, we could take him to the cleaners. Like a fool I said I don't want his money, what I want is a written apology.

As I have said before, he is a very uneducated man and has to have somebody else write his letters for him, so he can copy it out in his own handwriting. So it was obvious she had written it for him. It read it is none of our business who she sees and who she sleeps with. He then hand delivered it to me. "You call this an apology?" I asked, "Well, I'm taking this to the solicitor and let her take you to the cleaners as she suggested." He panicked and said, "What do you want me to write?" "The truth," I said, "and I want you to name all these so called men, I've supposed to have been with. If I ever hear you have slandered my name again, I will personally show these men your letter, and let them deal with you." I still have his letter to this day,

Not long afterwards, there was a charity dance held in the City Hall in aid of the Heart Foundation. My sister Janet and I decided to go. I knew my children would be there, so we all sat together. Shortly after, Terry and Pauline walked in. Before I knew it, my children were over to their table like bees round a honey pot. As you can imagine I was furious. I berated them saying, "How can you have anything to do with a woman who told lies about your mother; unless you believe her." My eldest daughter replied, "She's going to be our step-mother so we have to be nice to her." "Fine," I said "well you don't need two mothers," and stomped off. "Well, it's your loss." she replied and I never saw them again, for many months. I was broken hearted but stubborn. Even after all these years, I will never forgive that woman for coming between my children and myself.

Several months later there was a knock on my door. I answered it and to my surprise, it was my three daughters. "What do you want?" I asked. "May we come in or will you throw us out?" they asked. "I did not throw you out in the first place, it was your choice but don't expect me to forgive you," I replied. Then it all came out that she treated them like outcasts. Their father was not allowed to see them. They were not welcome. My answer was, "serve you right. You thought she was so wonderful." Being a mum I let it go, but I have never forgotten the hurt.

All of a sudden he took to visiting me to see if I were all right. I actually felt sorry for him, being under the thumb of this ghastly woman. To my great shame I started to have feelings for him. I became a phone stalker. I phoned him at all hours. On one of his visits, I told him I could not live without him; I even asked him to make love to me. His answer was "yuck I don't want you." That was the best favour he ever did me. It woke me up from whatever delusion I was under It must have given him great satisfaction because the first thing he did was he and his girl friend went to see my eldest daughter, they told her to go and see your mother; she is going to commit suicide. This was the furthest thing form my mind. I will admit, I was distraught at the insult and was crying when they arrived. It was a cruel thing to do to his daughter, particularly as my daughter and her family were at the local swimming baths enjoying a family afternoon. So he spoilt it for them because they all rushed over to see if I was alright. This was 1986. I spent the next year feeling very sorry for myself.

After I moved house in April of 1983, I started receiving some rather large gas bills. I knew they must be wrong as the only gas I used was heating and hot water; everything else was electric. So by the end of the summer, I queried it. All they ever did was to come and read the meter and then send me an even bigger bill. This went on for over a year. They were charging me hundreds of pounds even during the summer when there was no gas being used, except the pilot light. We had heated exchanges, but it got me nowhere.

In desperation, I spoke to one of our councillors; May Kiddle, and she got in touch with the Department of Energy. The Department of Energy got in touch with the Gas Board and told them they wanted to check the meter. The Gas Board wrote me a very nasty letter saying they had to change the meter and if the meter was found not to be faulty, they were going to charge me for it. The Department of Energy came and took the old meter away and tested it. They later wrote me to say the meter was erroneous and that they would be getting in touch with the Gas Board. When I finally heard from the Gas Board, I received a rebate of three pounds but no apology, after taking hundreds of pounds from me. I also used to pay a yearly insurance to cover parts and a yearly service. Each year the service would be later and later, so I ended up paying for a yearly service and they would turn up every fifteen months or so. When I decided, to sell up and move into sheltered accommodation in 2001, I wrote to the Gas Board to cancel my account. They told me to read my meter and send it to them in writing, which I did. I had just paid my January bill and I moved on the 12th of February, so there should not have been much to pay. When I left the house, I made sure I turned the gas off at the mains. After I moved I received an enormous gas bill of about £350. I disputed this. The letters got nasty and they even threatened to take me to court. Luckily, I don't roll over and die for anybody. I got in touch with the Citizens Advice Bureau and took all the bills and correspondence with me. By then the bills had reached four hundred pounds. Thankfully they were able to sort it out for me. I ended up paying £35. It makes me wonder if they just pick on old people, or do they just pick a number.

In 1987 I decided to shake myself out of the doldrums and get on with my life; I wanted to go dancing again. Although we met at a dance; during our marriage we very rarely went dancing unless I made the arrangements and paid for the tickets, usually on my birthday or our wedding anniversary. If he knew there was anything I enjoyed, he made sure we did not do it and in the twenty six years that we were married, I saw every New Years Eve in on my own with the T.V.

I knew my old friend David Ford ran a dancing class so I decided to join. Although I could get around the floor reasonably well, I had always wanted to learn to do it properly. I phoned many times to try to enrol but I always got a negative response. There was always some excuse why I could not, like the class was full and would I try again next term. Terry used to belong to David's school. I knew which days he used to go, so I made sure I booked for a different day, but the answer was still no. So I decided to forget about it. Then I received a prospectus from the college. I looked through it and discovered that they were advertising for students in David's class, and being a determined sort of person, I applied. I paid my fee to the college for the term and was told the starting date would be the 17th of October, on a Friday. I started the term on the 17th of October 1987. When I arrived I got a very chilly reception, but I was there to learn to dance so I did not take much notice. The following Friday things thawed out a bit except David's wife decided she did not like me. I had no idea why at the time; I did not know her and she did not know me. Any way she was always very unkind. Maybe she thought that if she upset me enough, I would leave, but I'm just as strong willed as she was, so I stuck it out.

I used to live in Wilton and had to come in by bus. A few weeks down the line, I was offered a lift by one of the ladies, Muriel Crisp; "I like you," she said, "We were expecting a real horror. We were all warned, by David's wife, to expect trouble." I was quite taken aback and wondered why she would say such a thing when I had never done her any harm. But I soldiered on as I thought that if I left, I would be the loser and she would have won. The following week during our coffee break I was sitting next to Muriel chatting and the lady who partnered Muriel, Dorothy Keating by name, went up to fetch their coffees. Muriel said to me "I've just realised who you are. You are married to Terry Blake, aren't you? I dance with him on Mondays. I think I've heard him mention you sometimes." I replied that I was married and we had been divorced for almost eight years. Just then Dorothy, who was returning from getting the coffees, overheard the tail end of our conversation. "No, no," she cried, "whatever you do, don't have anything to do with that man. He's feckless, unreliable and he's brought more women to this hall than I can count. You are far too nice for him." "I know," I said, "I was married to him for twenty six years." she put her hand to her mouth in embarrassment and said "I'm sorry, I'm sorry." "You weren't to know," I said.

They ran classes at St. Edmund's School at Laverstock on Monday, at St. Francis Church hall on Tuesday, Wednesday, Thursday and Friday at Sarum 76 in Brown St and elsewhere at the weekend. I stuck to Friday for several months till I felt more confident then I started to attend the Tuesday class and loved every minute of it. I never had a partner of my own, so I used to dance with either David or Angela; both of whom were brilliant dancers. I did not mind which because I knew I would have a good partner, also the other ladies would share their partners with me, so I very rarely had to sit any dances out. All in all, I found every one very charming. The following spring, there was to be a dance medals exam David asked me if I would like to take part. I declined, saying I didn't feel I was ready and that I didn't wish to make a fool of myself. "You won't," he said, "you are very good." I still said no, maybe next time.

That autumn they started a sequence dance class on a Thursday It was some Australian thing, anyway I joined and after our class there was a ballroom class. I used to leave the hall about seven to catch my bus home, but the weather was turning cold and my bus did not arrive till half past.

So one evening I asked David if I could sit there until it was time for my bus. He said yes and I moved to the other end of the class so as not to get in the way of the other dancers. Everybody else in the class was there and suddenly the door opened and Terry stood poised in the doorway saying, ta-dah I'm here.' he was always a bit of a show off, and then he spotted me. He came over and said, "What are you doing here?" "Waiting for a bus actually," I replied and as it was almost time to catch my bus, I left.

He didn't turn up the following Thursday and while I was sitting there, David asked me if I would care to dance. "But I don't belong to this class," I said. "That's alright," he replied, "you can have one dance before you catch your bus." it was a quick step I remember. "You are very good," he said, "have you ever thought of doing ballroom?" "I would love to do ballroom but I can't be in the same class as Terry, it wouldn't work." "Well it's up to you, as long as you promise, there won't be trouble, he said. "You won't get any from me," I replied, "but I can't speak for him."

The following Thursday, he asked "why have you joined my class" "It isn't your, class I said any one can join". From then on he made a point of asking me to dance. His intention was to embarrass me on the floor. He knew all the footwork but he was a terrible lead. He would pick fault and when we got to the other side of the room, he would call out loudly, "David, would you come and show my partner what she's doing wrong." luckily, David was watching like a hawk. He would come over and say "do it again and let me see for myself." We would go over it again and David would say, "It's not her Terry, it's you." Terry then said, "I must be getting old." I smiled very sweetly and replied, "Yes!" From then on to my relief, he stopped asking me to dance.

After a while he started to come to the Friday class and brought one of his many mistresses with him. Her name was Shirley. She made a point of sitting next to me. She introduced herself and then proceeded to tell me that I should not be in Terry's dancing school and that I should leave and join another dancing school. "What on earth has it got to do with you or Terry for that matter?" I asked, "He doesn't own the school and I'll go where I please." A few weeks down the line she came and sat beside me again and said, "I really do like you, you know," to which I replied, "I really couldn't care less." "Oh! I do hope so," she said, "I think you are a very nice person." After that she was always nice to me and started coming on her own.

10

The following spring I decided to go in for my medals. The first level was bronze, so I asked David if I could have a few private lessons to make sure I was good enough to pass. He agreed and after a few lessons he said I should go for both bronze and silver, as I was good enough. So I took Sequence, Modern, Latin and Old Time. I had good marks and I was very proud of myself. I also took bronze in Ballroom.

David said he was very pleased with me and said that next time I could do gold in Sequence and silver in Ballroom which included the Viennese waltz, without the fleckels, my marks were good and I was pleased with myself. Dancing had become the love of my life. David then asked me if I would help him with a few of his teaching classes, as his wife no longer wanted to help more than three days a week. I agreed because it would give me more experience and of course, I loved to dance. I was still having a private lesson once a week, in readiness for my gold medals. It was just ballroom but this time including Latin, Tango and the Viennese waltz with fleckels. It was hard work, but I loved it. He insisted on being technically correct. We had become very close, working together; we had known each other since I was eighteen and the bond between us felt natural, but it was no more than that.

It was April of 1989 and we were getting ready for the gold medal exams. He was complaining about my rumba. He said I wasn't putting any oomph into it. "You are too inhibited. Use those hips, he said, "it isn't dirty it's supposed to be sensuous. I want to see you move those hips in a figure of eight." Well I gave it all I had and he suddenly stopped and said "Steady on, mind my blood pressure!" I burst out laughing and so did he and before I knew it he'd taken me in his arms and I didn't even try to fight it, nor did I feel guilty. We became lovers until he became ill about a year before he died of leukaemia. He did tell me that our affair couldn't lead to any thing. He'd been divorced twice and married three times and he couldn't go through all that again, "Nobody asked you, sir she said", quoting from a children's rhyme, "you are not exactly marriage material, with your track record." "Cheeky bitch," he replied. "No," I said, "I have the best of both worlds. I'm happy the way things are." Our relationship lasted almost thirteen years and I don't regret a moment of it. He would not let me see him during his illness. He wanted me to remember him as he was but we would phone each other once a week and if I was a day or two late, he wanted to know where I was and why I hadn't phoned. When he died I was devastated. I did go to the funeral and found it difficult to hide my feelings. I didn't feel like dancing for a long time after that, but people were asking questions. So I went back, but I never really enjoyed it anymore. I will remember David forever. Those were the happiest years of my life.

In the early nineties I was called upon to do jury service. I thought it would be for about a week, but it stretched out for three. I certainly had my eyes opened about the legal system. On one occasion after waiting till eleven o'clock, we were summoned to the court by the judge and dismissed because the prisoner, who was travelling from Wales hadn't woken up in time. I also discovered that solicitors are very dishonest people. I heard them many times, apologising to the judge for misleading them. This was after all their client's other crimes were read out. I came to the conclusion that the law is an ass. I have proven it is so. Many times I have called the police out when my home was vandalised by certain teenagers. Living in an end of terrace house and living alone, I was fair game. Mostly the police never turned up. On one occasion at eleven thirty in the evening, I rang the police and was told they couldn't spare anyone, but if the boys were still there in five minutes, ring again. I rang five minutes later and they said by the time we get there, the boys will have run away. "What are you waiting for?" I asked, for me to be robbed, raped or murdered." I put my dressing gown on and went out myself and said to the boys, "Do your parents know you are out? And where are they? In the pub, no doubt I said. With that they slunk off.

The following day when I got home from work I found the trellis torn down from the wall. It was obvious they were getting their revenge. In a rage, I phoned the police yet again. "I want the police here now and I don't want any excuses," I said. A policeman arrived and I showed him the damage. I also told him about the events of the night before. He swore to me the message had not been reported. "You are the sixth person to complain" he said, "The trouble is we have civilian telephonists and they won't report anything, because it means, writing it in triplicate." "Why then do you employ them?" I asked, "because of government cuts," he replied.

I complained to the mother of one of these boys. All she said was, "you are a miserable old bag. You are spoiling my son's fun." After several months of misery, I attended the monthly Council meeting and stated my case. I also told them about the drug dealers who pulled up in the car park behind my house. "Oh! No," they said, "it does not happen in Wilton." I went to two more meetings with the same result. Luckily at the last meeting, the press were there along with the police. "I will prove that there are drug dealers," I said. "I will take down all the car numbers and give it to you." "Please be careful," they said, "don't let them see you." "But you said it does not happen in Wilton," I replied. Well, the upshot was that after I gave them the car numbers, five people were arrested. The following week there was a report in the local paper about this poor old lady and all she had to put up with. They did not give my name or address, but it was obvious to me who they were talking about. The next thing I knew, reporters from different newspapers were phoning for an interview. I replied that I had said all I'm going to say on the matter. Then GMTV phoned and I gave them the same answer. Then they said that I owed it to myself and other people of my age to speak out. The next thing I knew my sitting room was filled with cameras, lights and interviewers and I had my five minutes of fame on the six o'clock news. Most people said I was very brave to stand up to the thugs, others had a different opinion.

My daughter Carol lived in a lovely bungalow just around the corner from me, which was very nice, but she spent most of her time in my house. She probably meant well, but as I was still working, I had no time to myself to do all the things I needed to do. One day I said to her, "Haven't you got a home to go to?" She took umbrage at that, so I said you could be doing your own housework, instead of preventing me from doing mine. On one of her visits, my grandson, Matthew, who was two at the time, asked me if he could have some grapes from the fruit bowl. I took half a dozen, removed the stalks, (they were seedless) and gave them to him. He put the lot into his mouth all at once and started to choke. He stopped breathing and was turning blue. Carol became hysterical and poked her fingers down his throat, making things worse. She started crying. I snatched him from her, turned him upside down and gave him a sharp bang on the back and the grape, shot right across the room. Thank God, for my first aid training. Then I yelled at him, for being a greedy boy.

Around about 1998 or maybe earlier, a woman called Gill Carter joined one of our dance classes. She did not have a partner of her own, so I had to dance as man with her; she was a very pleasant lady and we got on well. It was the same class that Terry used and he brought many different partners, but none of them stayed long.

One day he arrived without a partner so he thought that I would have to dance with him. I told him I could not dance with both of them, so they would have to dance together.

The next week he complained, "I can't dance with her, she's doing my bloody back in". "I'm sorry I said, you have no choice this is not my class, I just help David. I can't leave you sitting and I can't leave Gill sitting, so you will have to make the best of it." The following week it was quite obvious that it was more than dancing going on. A few weeks down the line, there was a knock on my door. It was Terry. "Yes, what is it?" I asked. "I thought I would come and tell you myself, he said, before you hear it from anyone else; but I'm moving in, with Gill and renting my flat out." "What has it got to do with me?" I asked, "We have been divorced for eighteen years, just one thing, don't treat her like you treated me, she's a nice woman". "She is a nice woman, he replied; she has four bank accounts and stocks and shares." I was astounded that he could be so mercenary. He moved into her house in Lower Bemerton. After a while they sold her house and moved to a cottage in Sixpenny Handley where they lived till his death about a year ago; but I'm delighted to say she wore the trousers. He now did all the things he never did for me housework, gardening, shopping, everything he never did in his life before. He often complained to our eldest daughter about this and that and she tells me about it. My reply is always the same "it couldn't happen to a nicer person". My daughter doesn't approve of how I feel about her father, but she will have to learn to live with it. The pain of what I went through with him goes too deep to be erased. I can't understand her loyalty to him, when so many times he's denied being her father.

I have no problem with Gill. She is just what he needed or deserves. I love it when he had to do as he was told. She has invited me along with my family at Christmas on occasion. But it irritated me to see him making faces at her behind her back while she was telling him to do something. Eventually, I declined her invitation and when she asked me why, I said "the less I see of him the better."

The only one of his children he ever bothered to visit is the eldest girl Carol. When my youngest daughter's partner said to him one Christmas, "I think we will have to get you one of those gadgets to fit in your car so you can find your way to our house." "What do I need one of those for?" he asked. "Well! You always visit Carol, but never Trish. You should not play favourites." "I have no favourites," he replied, "I hate them all equally." He has always been sarcastic, but he thinks it's clever.

Gill takes him on holiday three or four times a year; to Canada to see her sister, to Scotland, to the Continent, all over the place. He knows he's on to a good thing, but he will get his comeuppance, one day. They do say, what goes round, comes round.

Gill has been very helpful to me from time to time. She has made him do odd jobs for me, things he has not or would not do, under normal circumstances. Once he cleared out and painted my guttering and he also artexed the ceiling in my sitting room. He said he did not want paying but I made sure I paid him although, it was a nominal payment, of about £25 and, of course, I supplied the materials. I was not going to be beholden to him. She also advised me on how to get back my endowment insurance which I was wrongly advised to take out by the mortgage lenders. So all in all, I had a lot to be grateful to her for.

The years went by and I started buying my house, in 1985 I believe. It was a hard struggle, paying the mortgage and the bills, so I had to get rid of my car because I couldn't afford both. I worked in a department called Metals for thirteen years. I was also on the first aid team. I also made some very good friends, whom I still keep in touch with. All in all it was a very happy thirteen years. Of course, you get the odd ones who are disagreeable, but I suppose that's normal wherever you go. The only thing I wasn't happy about was the smoking. It affected my breathing. I had several attacks of bronchitis; one attack was serious enough to have me rushed to hospital and have me put into an oxygen tent. I was very relieved when the ban on smoking came into force.

In the last year before my retirement we were taken over by another firm. The new manager was acting like a new broom and was quite ruthless. I had the feeling he was trying to get rid of all the people of retiring age. He moved these people into jobs he knew we were not able to do; it was either do the job or leave. He moved me to a department he knew I could not cope with. It meant standing all day and lifting heavy weights, both of which I wasn't able to do. He knew this because not only did I tell him, but it was in my records that I had osteoarthritis of the spine. He said, no, you'll be alright. So I struggled for a few weeks. He came in every day saying "Good morning, Patricia, and how, are we this morning" "In a lot of pain, thank you," I replied. "Good, good," he said, "see you tomorrow." One day while I was lifting some heavy trays on to some shelves in the dungeon, I felt my back crack and I was in terrible pain. I went to see the nurse to report it. All she said was, "Are you telling me the truth?" To which I replied "If that siren went now, I would not be able to walk to the accident, let alone run." Well if that's all they care, I thought, I had better see my doctor.

The doctor examined me and told me I had to have complete bed rest for two weeks, then go back and see him. I went back after the two weeks and he asked me how I was feeling. "A bit better," I replied. "Are you sure you want to go back there?" he asked "I'm perfectly willing to sign you off till you retire and they will have to pay your wages for thirteen weeks." He told me he wrote to them and told them that I could not do that kind of work at my age. They had replied and he asked if I would like to read it. "I don't trust them," he said. I read the letter which stated that they would be happy to see Mrs Blake back and we will make sure she will not be going back to that department. I said to my doctor, I would like to go back and retire with a bit of dignity, to which he replied, "Blow your dignity, unless you want to retire in a wheelchair."

I went back for a week. On the first morning I had to see the personnel manager. I asked her if I was going back to Metals, "Certainly not," she said, "you will be going back to the factory, but on a different job." It was different but just as strenuous and after a week of pain, I went back to my doctor. He asked me to describe what I was doing and when I showed him, he said, "You're never going back there. I am going to sign you off until you retire, and let them pay your wages." But the damage done to my back was irreversible; it ruined the rest of my life in respect of not being able to do all the physical things I used to do.

My doctor sent me to see a specialist at the General Hospital; He gave me about ten minutes of his time. He didn't talk to me rather, he talked about me to a colleague in my presence and when he was done discussing all my defects, he turned to me and said, "What do you expect at your age? And don't try and sue because backs are hard to prove." Dr Brown then referred me to Dr. Robertson, who as it turned out, was a great help to me. He did a lot of tests, MRI scans and things. he then told me there was nothing he could do except teach me how to live with it, how to sit, stand, lie down, anything to make my life more comfortable and it was he who encouraged me to write this book. When my mother went into hospital for the last time he asked me how she was; as she was a patient of his. I told him she was in hospital and it was unlikely she would ever leave. "I'm sorry to hear that," he said, "you have a lovely mother." "You have no idea," I replied, "she hasn't got a maternal bone in her body and I burst into tears. So; after asking me a few questions, he then said, "write about it and maybe it will heal you." It took me more than five years to think about it because I felt it would be disloyal. But, in the end I thought, why not? Instead of letting it eat into me, I shall.

Early in 2000, after a visit to Vancouver I went to see my doctor. "What can I do for you?" he asked. "The sight in my right eye has gone peculiar, I said, I can see round the periphery, but not in the middle." This was early in March. "I will write to the eye specialist, at the hospital he said and get him to make you an appointment."About three months later I had to visit my doctor about something completely unrelated and the doctor asked if I had heard from the hospital about my eye. "No," I said. "What!" he exclaimed, "three months is the outside limit." With that he phoned the hospital and asked why I had not heard. The secretary simply said, Mrs Blake's notes are still in the in tray, we only look at these things when we have the time. I finally got an appointment about seven weeks later.

When I saw the specialist and he checked my eye, he said, "you have macular degeneration and there's nothing we can do about it. Naively I asked; "what caused it?" "Old age, of course he said, anyway, you have one good eye, what more do you want?" "Two, if you don't mind, I replied I'm not satisfied with your prognosis; I would like a second opinion." "Fine," he said and wrote to Southampton. They took no time at all to send me an appointment. I saw a Mr Andrews, who agreed it was a hole in the retina, but it could be repaired. "Why did Salisbury say nothing could be done?" I asked. He merely shrugged his shoulders. They did the repair on the 8th October 2000 and said it would only be a 95% success. If I had come earlier, it would have been a 100%.

My brother Denzil had to go into the same hospital on the same day to have a biopsy on his lungs. Earlier, he had had a heart attack and when he had a scan they discovered a shadow on his lung. It turned out to be cancer. They decided to operate, on the 21st November. He phoned me the weekend before and told me he was never going home, he did not want to go home. I became angry and told him not to talk such rubbish, if he didn't fight this thing, he would die. "I want to die," he said, "I would rather die than go home." he gave me lots of reasons why not and I am filled with guilt for being angry with him. I told him I would phone the hospital after his operation to see how he was. The nurse who answered asked who I was. "His sister," I replied, she told me he had just come back from theatre and I could phone the following day. The next day when I phoned, the nurse was rather abrupt. "Who are you and what do you know about it?" I said "I'm his sister and I phoned yesterday." "Well, he is in a coma and has been moved to the intensive care ward and not to come to see him as his family has barred me and it's more than their job's worth to let me in." I then phoned my sister-in-law and asked why, she merely said "No in-laws, just family." "But I'm his sister for God's sake; I'm closer to him than you are, If I haven't heard from you, by Saturday, I'm going up whether you like it or not." Saturday morning came and the phone rang. It was my sister-in-law who said as soon as I picked up the phone that Denzil had died at five o'clock this morning, and she put the phone down. I was hysterical. I phoned her again and my nephew answered. "She doesn't want to talk to you," he said. I phoned my second daughter and asked her to take me to see my brother's body. He was in the mortuary and I almost did not recognise him, he was so bloated. Apparently, his kidneys had stopped working. He died on 2nd December 2000 and his funeral was on 13th December. Two of my daughters my niece and myself, attended the funeral in the West End Church, Southampton. We sat in the third row from the front, leaving the two front rows for the family. When they arrived they all crowded into the first row although they could hardly fit. They left the second row empty. Any one would think that we had something contagious.

As we left the church, I saw the hearse drive away. I asked my sister in law "Where is Den going?" "To the undertakers," she replied. "Are we not going with him?" I asked. "No, we are going to the pub for food." "What is going to happen to Den?" I asked, "We are going to wait for the better weather, then we are going to have him interred somewhere nice". "Don't forget to let me know when and where, because I would like to be there." I waited and waited, but nobody got in touch, so I started to phone, but no one would answer; January, February and March went by and still no news. Eventually I phoned my nephew Stephen, in Wales. "It's been four months now, I said, when are you going to lay your dad to rest?" "We did it on the third of March, he replied, on his birthday." "Why did you not tell me, you knew I wanted to be there?" "Mum said no, she did not want any in-laws." "If you didn't have the decency to let me be there, at least have the decency to let me know where he is buried." "I can't remember," he said. "What do you mean, you can't remember, you were there, were you not?" "Well, mum doesn't want you to know, I will have to ask her." It took two days for him to get back to me and when he did, it was a very vague, somewhere in West End.

The following Tuesday, I went up by bus and searched high and low. There were three cemeteries, as I recall but I could not find him. I wasn't going to give up, so I got in touch with the vicar of our local church. They finally found him; there wasn't even a marker on his grave. About a year later there was a stone. I go and tidy his grave two or three times a year. My youngest daughter, Trish and her partner, Kerry, take me as I'm not as mobile as I used to be. Sadly, although my brother's family live five or ten minutes away, I very rarely see any evidence of them visiting.

11

On my sixtieth birthday, 18th May 1995, I received the usual cards and presents from my children and friends. But it was just, another day, it did not feel special no celebration, no party. I just felt a bit neglected. I know it was silly, but I was hurt.

The following week or so, my friends at the dancing class asked me if, I had had a party for my retirement "no" I said. They were quite surprised. "It's not that important," I lied and left it at that. A couple of weeks after that, Stan and Betty, a couple who lived in Durrington invited me and another couple for tea and biscuits one afternoon. I was picked up by my friends Pam and Jim Hopkins. We drove to a lovely bungalow. It was a hot sunny day in June and we had tea on the lawn. As the afternoon drew on I noticed a few more couples drifting in. I began to wonder what was going on. Suddenly around five o'clock, Betty asked us all to come indoors. There in the dining room was a spread fit for a king. It still didn't dawn on me that it was for my benefit until the cards and presents were brought out. I was so overcome that I burst into tears; to think that strangers had done for me what my own family had not.

I did not say anything to my family till a couple of years later, when my eldest daughter asked me to make her father a cake for his retirement on his 65th birthday on 21st July. I was outraged as it made me feel second best. She even offered to pay me for making it. She gave him a lovely party on the lawn. I was invited and I went, but I was seething inside.

When it was my birthday, the following year, she rang me to ask if I could baby sit for her, at about 3.30pm. I said that I would. She said she would ring me when she was ready. 3.30 came, then 4 o'clock and still no phone call. So I thought I would go over as perhaps she was running late. She is always late for everything. In fact, I have told her many a time, that on the day of her funeral she would be chasing the hearse down the road shouting "Wait for me!"

When I arrived, I went round to the back door and found everyone scuttling about trying to hide things. Then my daughter shouted at me saying "You've spoilt the surprise!" She had gone to a lot of trouble to get all my family together, sisters, brother and mother, one of my other children and family. She had also invited Terry and Gill. Everyone was dressed in their best and I was dressed in my old clothes ready for babysitting. I was not amused. I turned round and went back home. My youngest daughter's partner, Kerry, came after me and persuaded me to get changed and return.

Carol, my eldest thought I was being ungrateful. I told her I felt she was only doing it because she had put her father first. It felt like a booby prize. To make matters worse when my son-in-law suggested that we should get the family together so that he could film it, Terry replied "Oh Stephen, I didn't know you were into horror movies!" That finished it for me.

After I moved to Sarah Hayter's sheltered accommodation in Salisbury, I continued, to go dancing for as long as I could, but it became increasingly painful with the spine deteriorating. Eventually I had to admit defeat and had to give it up. I then discovered the U3A or the University of the Third Age where men and women of retiring age can join classes of various sorts different languages, IT, water colours, writing, card making, all sorts; one need never be bored. I do two art classes, French, creative writing, I have done IT and photography. I don't have time to be bored. Sometimes I feel I have over stretched myself, but it's better than looking at the four walls.

I went to college when I retired to learn sugar craft and thoroughly enjoyed it. I have learned many skills and from time to time, I make celebration cakes to order, wedding cakes, birthday, anniversary or whatever is requested.

I have flown to Vancouver seven times to visit relatives, so I have had quite a few adventures. My latest trip was to New Zealand to my second daughter's second wedding in Timaru on the South Island. I loved every moment and did not want to come home. I think my travelling days are at an end now. I don't think I can cope with the stress of travelling any more, unless it's first class; cheap flights are very uncomfortable.

One Saturday, about six summers ago in August I believe, I went down town to do my shopping. I went into T.K. Max, to shop for some new under wear. While I was in there I was mugged by two teenage girls. Nobody saw anything because there were no cameras in that part of the store. I saw the manager, but he could not help. I got home as soon as I could and phoned the police. All I got was an answer phone and it took three hours for them to get back to me. Nobody came to see me and it took a month, before I received a letter from them saying, I'm sorry to hear you were a victim of crime and would I like some counselling; they also gave me a crime number.

The following January I had a phone call from a woman purporting to be from the police telling me my handbag had been found and would I give her details of what was in my bag; she even gave me a fake, crime number. I had an uneasy feeling about this, so I said I know I'm nearly seventy one, but I'm not senile yet. When she rang off, I tried the 1471 number to check but they had withheld the number. I then rang the real police and told them what had happened. All they said was, I hope you did not give them any information, that's not even the right crime number; so I repeated what I had already said to the other woman. This is another reason why I don't have any faith in the police.

Over these last few years I have had a few health problems, one of those being high blood pressure; but the medication, did not agree with me. I must be allergic to it because I have been rushed into A and E several times, with anaphylactic shock. I can't speak too highly of the department. I have had the best of care and it was they who discovered what was causing the problem.

My doctor, Dr Brown is one of the best and I trust him implicitly. He is not one to put a prescription in your hand on every visit, he looks into things before writing a prescription. Anyway, after trying three different medications, I decided to take myself off everything because I feel much better without the drugs. I know he won't give up on me till he finds something suitable.

The first week in January 2000, I received a phone call from my youngest sister; I was surprised as we never had anything to do with one another. She said "Thank you for the Christmas card, sorry I didn't send you one." "Not a problem," I said "I just send to every body on the list, no big deal." She then started crying, "I've never been a good sister to you have I?" "No, you have not," I replied. She sounded rather drunk. "I need your forgiveness," she said. "If you mean," I replied, "I have to forgive you for sleeping with my husband, then, no, I will never forgive you; sisters don't do that sort of thing to each other." She cried some more and I hung up.

A couple of years later she rang and asked if she could come and visit me; apparently she was having a free holiday with some charity to

Bournemouth. She was always on benefits; that is how she lived. I agreed to meet her at the bus station with a wheel chair. We had lunch and then I took her back to the bus. She used to live in Worcester, she then sold her house for about £125,000, and then she bought a cottage in Wales for about £75,000. She then had the cheek to ask me how much money she could have in the bank without losing her benefits. "Don't ask me," I said, "I have always worked for my living." Weeks later, she phoned and said "All that stuff I told you about Terry and me, I did not sleep with Terry." "Don't you think it's a bit late for you to deny all that," I said, "I have always known about it." After a long pause she said, "I don't regret it, I enjoyed it," and put the phone down.

In December of 2001, I went to Vancouver to spend Christmas with my sister Janet and her third husband, Fay Roset. They gave me a great time, but I was not impressed with him. He was generous and all that, but he disrespected my sister, he spoke to her like dirt. He made fun of how peeled a banana, he told her only monkeys ate like that. She had to learn to drive because his sight was failing, he had Diabetes; he would shout at her if she used the rear view mirror he said if he caught her using it he would say I'm' going to rip it out; use the wing mirrors I was amazed that she took it from him; I got angry and told him off. I told him the rear view mirrors were there for a purpose and you are legally obliged to use it. He was very free with the F. word, which I hate to hear. He was not a well man and she made excuses for him, so I let it ride. One morning at breakfast the phone rang, it was my sister Geraldine; Janet put the phone on loudspeaker so everyone could join in the conversation. I of course, did not join in. After a long chat Geraldine, said her goodbyes and said give my love to Fay. Then Jan said what about Trish, to which Geraldine replied, "if you must." she obviously did not realise I could hear the conversation. One morning at breakfast, when he was berating my sister, about something petty; I reacted and lost my temper and told him what I thought of him. I had two weeks left of my holiday but I could not stand a minute more, so I told my sister I was leaving; I phoned my cousin and asked if I could stay with him till my flight; I packed my things and asked my sister to drive me there. Janet's husband said "I have friends in high places and I'll make sure you'll, never be allowed into this country again"; I replied, "like you have that much power".

It seems that I always get sent for whenever Jan is in trouble. She lost her husband I think it was in 2003 in November. I wasn't able to travel at that time, so I told her I would come as soon as I could which was early in February 2004. Apparently the step daughter, was about to evict her from the apartment she shared with her husband. In his will Jan was supposed to live out her days there. "That's not going to happen", said the step daughter. She destroyed all his papers, so Jan didn't have a leg to stand on.

When I arrived, it was 7° below zero. The daughter, who lived in the apartment upstairs, turned all the heat off to make it as uncomfortable as possible for us. We stuck it out as long as we could, we then found an eviction notice pinned to the front door. We had no choice, so we asked one of our cousins, Neville, to put us up until she found a place of her own. It was very stressful and hard work, seeing that both my sister and I were in advancing years. It was then that I realised that my sister had not changed a bit; everything was still all about her and her feelings. My feelings did not count. She would scream and shout at me for the slightest thing. I put it down to grief and stress, till one day she screamed at me for disturbing her afternoon nap; I had no idea she had gone to bed. I said she ought to go back to bed; she was standing there in her bra and pants. She just got back to her bedroom, when the phone rang. I answered it, it was her friend Sharon. "Can I speak to Jan?" she asked. "She is resting," I replied, "can I get her to call you back?" the next thing I knew, Jan was taking the phone out of my hand. She very sweetly said, "Hi, Sweetie"! That did it, I exploded. "How dare you treat me like you do, I did not spend my time and money coming to be with you, for you to talk to me like that." With that she burst into tears, threw her arms round my neck and said "I'm still grieving, I'm sorry."

I believe it was October 2006, when the youngest sister died. She was riddled with cancer and other problems. Janet could not afford the plane fare to come over, so one of Geraldine's sons paid for her to come. She phoned me from the boy's house and asked me to rent the guest room in the almshouse where I live for a couple of weeks, to which I agreed. "But don't expect me to come to the funeral. I am not a hypocrite." She arrived after the funeral and did not spend a single day with me, except the two days we spent with our cousin, Hilary, in Haywards Heath in Sussex. Each day, she would rise between nine and ten have her breakfast, then I would not see her again till her evening meal. It cost her nothing, I paid for her room and her food because I knew she could not afford it. I was very hurt that she treated me as a convenience, as I always paid my way when I stayed with her in Canada. On her last day her daughter Debbie, her husband and myself saw her off to the train station. When the train arrived, she got on the train without a backward glance, no goodbye, thank you, nothing. I shouted after her, "Hey!" So she got off the train, walked back and said, "Thanks for everything." and was gone She didn't even phone to say she arrived home safely, till two weeks later.

Every time I visited her in Canada, she was always charming to me in front of other people, but when we were on our own, it was another matter; she snipped and snapped and shouted. Every thing had to be about her. I was told everything on a need to know basis, usually about ten minutes before we had to leave; so if I was not ready, it was something else to moan about. My last visit was the 20th June 2007. I had intended to go a bit later but my cousin Thelma, phoned to ask me to come earlier, as they were going to visit her eldest daughter and her husband, who lived at Fraiser Lakes. I agreed and booked my flight. I then phoned my sister. I was taken aback with her reply. "Oh! She said, I thought it was going to be just Thelma and me" she said, "I need a holiday." "Fine," I said, "if you feel like that, I will stay in your flat by myself, till you get back. It's too late to change my ticket."

When I arrived I discovered that my cousin had invited her youngest son and his wife along, which meant there was no room for a fifth passenger and my sister had to use her own car. So I paid for most of the petrol. It took two days to drive there and two days to drive back, stopping at a Motel for the night, which my cousin Thelma paid for. The heat was unbearable and we were eaten alive by black fly and mosquitoes. We stayed for about nine days, I was very glad to return to Vancouver. I had been quite ill for a few days. On our return journey to Vancouver; the heat was unbearable, so I wound the window down; "close it she said, it's too noisy," "well can you put the air conditioner on;" "no she said, I'm not getting cold feet for you". When we returned to her flat, I discovered she still had the youngest sister's ashes that she had brought back from England with her; she had promised she would get rid the ashes before I arrived. I was angry and said, "You have no respect for my feelings. After all she did to me, I don't wish to be under the same roof, dead, or not." "Well I liked her," she said, "feet of clay and all. I don't like you." There was more, to come.

The day before I was due to leave, I phoned the airport as one does, to check if the flight was still on. "You've missed your flight," they said. "Don't be silly," I replied, its' not due till tomorrow, the 27th July. I booked from the 20th June till the 27th of July. Why would I pay all that money for about three days? It's obviously a mistake made by the office." "It's your responsibility they said, to check the ticket." Well I admit, I should have checked, perhaps I'm too trusting and I had to pay to come back. My sister started shouting at me. "Don't speak to me like a school mistress speaking to an imbecile," I said. "But you are an imbecile!" she replied. Needless to say, I won't be going there again unless there is an emergency. I know I have my uses and I'm used to being the bottom of the pecking order but I have decided enough is enough.

When I sold my house in Wilton, to move into sheltered accommodation; I gave my children two thousand pounds each and after I furnished my new flat I put the rest into I.S.A's, and bought a few, premium bonds and when my aunty died, I sent my cousin one thousand pounds to help cover some of her outstanding debts. I was glad to be of some help. Janet complained, that she was fed up using her husband's dead wife's furniture; so I sent her five hundred pounds, to put towards a new three piece suite. The next time I went, she still had the same furniture; I asked what happened, she said she had backed into a neighbours car and done a thousand dollars worth of damage and she didn't want her husband to find out, so she paid it out of the money I gave her.

12

A lot has happened in the last seventeen years; I have been to Canada seven times,to New Zealand twice and Australia once, to visit a cousin; it was an interesting experience but it was much too hot and to get from A to B meant hours of driving, not for me of course, but for whom ever was doing the driving. I gave up driving years ago but it was still tiring.

I also met with a cousin in England, whom I had not seen for about sixty years and we get on like a house on fire. We are spookily alike and I'm very fond of her. Hilary and her husband Norman come to visit occasionally and we phone each other often.

There have been a few medical problems, over the years, one of them being, having to have a bladder repair. The surgeon was brilliant and did an excellent job. Unfortunately, they put me in a geriatric ward and the nursing there was abysmal; I know I should not be surprised, as it was like that, when my mother was a patient. I used to visit mum after work, it was usually supper time there would be patients calling out and asking for help, but the staff, male and female would be watching television and the only response was, hang on, wait. There was an old lady in the bed next to mothers, who could not feed herself, and as usual her food was left and taken away untouched, so mum used to get out of her bed and feed her. When the sister said something, mum asked her; "what makes you think you are a nurse, the uniform" my mother was a rubbish mother but she was a brilliant nurse. After my operation I was brought to the ward I had already been fitted with a catheter; when I noticed it was full I asked the nurse," shouldn't it be emptied;" "no she replied, bags of room"; then she went off duty. The night staff came on duty, and the nurse was a different kettle of fish; she was kind and caring; she was a Philippino, I think; she took one look at the overflowing catheter and said, "oh my goodness"; she emptied the bag and cleaned up the mess, I then asked her if I could have a mug of hot water to soak my dentures, "certainly she said no trouble."

The next morning, when the day staff came on duty, the unpleasant one with an attitude, shouted "get up, it's breakfast time" My bed was nearest the sink and as I could not get out of bed, while attached to the catheter, I asked, "could you please run the tap into this mug, to get rid of the steradent" she took the mug, put her hand in, took the teeth out and pushed them into my mouth, steradent and all; I was shocked.

There was an old lady, in the bed opposite me she was hallucinating, having jolly chats with an empty chair; in my opinion, it was because she was starved. They used to bring her meals and take it away untouched; she was too weak to feed herself

And nobody else would feed her.

The surgeon came to see me the following day, and told me he wanted me to stay in for four days. I said" no thank you," he asked why; "because I don't want to go home with more bugs than I came in with" He replied; "I don't blame you; if you can pee for me three times to my satisfaction, you can go home tonight". He called the nurse and told her to remove the packing inside me, so that I could take myself to the bathroom, to do the specimens. In two days, I did not even have a wash, although i had brought my wash things in with me.

That evening, before my daughter arrived to take me home, they decided to remove the I.V .from my hand, the nurse was rather rough, she put a dressing on the needle hole and walked away; blood started pouring, it ran down my arm and through my fingers and on to the floor so I called to the nurse, she turned and shouted, in an irritated voice; "WHAT". "I'm bleeding," I said; she turned to the ward sister, "sister, we have a bleeder here," with that there were three nurses at my side, one holding the pressure point one getting a new dressing and the third cleaning me and the floor with the same tissue.

The next morning after I got home, I got a phone call from my G.P; "are you all right Mrs. Blake"; "yes thank you" I replied, "why", "the hospital told me you have a urinary infection;" "would I know about it" I asked, "yes you would, it's very painful". "In that case I said, the specimen they gave you probably belonged to someone else."

Two or three years ago, I had a bad fall in the shower and banged my head. There was a lump about the size of an egg on the back of my head. I rang my surgery to ask their advise, they said "it's no use coming to the surgery; ring for an ambulance, if you don't we will."They were all very kind and I spent the whole day there having lots of tests, and they only let me go home, when they were quite satisfied that I was well enough to go home.

Shortly after that, I had a visit from the social services, they came to see if there was anything I needed; I told them, "I could do with a grab bar in the shower, to prevent my falling again" well it took about six months to get it but at least it was fixed, then a few days later a young lady visited and told me I was entitled to all kinds of services and she helped me get them; she was really helpful and I am most grateful.

Two years ago, I had a referral to the spinal doctor and after some scans and X-Rays they said I was to have an operation on my right shoulder. On my fourth appointment, they said they weren't going to bother, as my body was so riddled with osteoarthritis, that there was no point I was extremely angry but there was nothing I could do about it.

A couple of months later, I had a letter from the hospital, asking to see me on the tenth of May. I went up guns blazing I said "what do you want to see me for, you have already written me off." "No we haven't, we have been looking at your scans and X-Rays and discovered a lot of old injuries on your back and we would like to know how you got them." "That's easy I replied, I had a violent, brutal husband, he has blacked my eyes, broken my nose, knocked my teeth out albeit they were dentures, thrown me around the room by my hair and if I fell on the floor, he would put the boot in". "Sorry to hear that", he said; "well that's history" I said; so they then decided to operate. The surgeon did a great job, it was most uncomfortable being strapped up for six weeks, but it was worth it; I then had six injections in my spine but I'm sad to say, it has not made one iota of difference. Hopefully they might think of something else, in the meantime, I just have to grin and bear it. I was given a twelve week chart to write down the degrees of pain I was experiencing, and unfortunately it seems to have worsened.

There was no exact time when we realised that mum had some sort of dementia, but it must have been in her late fifties; she began to say and do strange things. She sometimes forgot to put certain ingredients in her cooking and then wonder why it did not taste the way it should; she would forget what she was saying half way through her sentence. She would get angry over nothing; we just thought she was being extra bloody minded, more than usual anyway. I had been looking after her since the late eighties after the family walked out on her, after a huge fight. She had said some terrible things to all of us and I don't blame them for leaving; I tried to reason with them, saying, you can't leave her. They told me, if you want to stay, more fool you.

She ranted and raved and told them to bugger off and you too she said to me; "don't be silly I said, why do you behave like this, you are your own worst enemy."

Shortly after she moved to a ground floor flat and the family came and helped her move and then it seemed, the family were back to normal; she obviously forgot the big row, but she became more strange, we tried to help her as much as possible in the physical sense I would go over every Saturday, take her shopping in the car and every Saturday as soon as we drove into the main car park she would ask, "where are we, I don't recognize this place are we lost" "no mum it's the main car park, we come here every week, "we would go back to her place and have to do her washing and hang it out to dry, I don't know who did her ironing, I assumed she did it herself, I had no idea of her mental state, I thought she was just being lazy, she always got away with doing as little as possible.

The kitchen sink was always full of dirty dishes, must have been a week's worth, she didn't even wash a cup.

The next job would be the garden, she expected the borders to be weeded and the grass cut. She had an electric mower and she would follow me, about six inches behind, flicking the lead with her cane I was terrified the lead would be cut and I would be electrocuted; I would tell her to sit down and let me get on with it and she would say "I'm only trying to help"; my whole Saturday morning was taken up doing her work.

Every Christmas I would have her over for the day, until she could no longer climb the stairs; after that I would have to go to her; this happened for eight years. One of those Christmases, she had Shingles and my son who decided to live with his father, got chicken pox so there was nothing for it but to cook the dinner and take it to both of them. I went to my son first and then to my mother, at the end of the day, when I got into my car to go home, the accelerator pedal fell off and I was stranded. I unpacked the food, into her fridge, walked to my daughter's in Salisbury and got them to take me home to Wilton.

The following day, Boxing day, I walked all the way from Wilton to Bishopdown in the freezing cold, about nine miles in all; it took me about an hour and a half ,I warmed the food and gave her, her dinner, she turned to me and said "this is the loneliest Christmas I have ever spent." I was really hurt; I said "and what am I Scotch mist?" after that I told my sister, it's about time she took a turn and she did for three years following.

Back in 1987 I believe we had a tornado and mum decided to go to the local shop, well the wind took her and she was thrown about, her spectacles were smashed and she looked like she had done ten rounds with Mike Tyson; she was black and blue; I suggested we try and get her into sheltered accommodation; she wouldn't hear of it, she then went around telling people I was trying to get rid of her; anyway we struggled on, it meant I had to go to her every evening to cook her a meal, prepare lunch for the next day and make sure she had whatever she needed.

This went on for several weeks I was tired and irritable and on one occasion when I called, I found her lying on her settee, fully dressed; overcoat and all I asked her where she had been, "to the hospital", she said "this time of night" I asked "no ten o'clock this morning."

I was so angry, I said, "so are you going to lie there and rot, why couldn't you get changed;" "if only I could;" she said. "What are you going to do, if I get ill who is going to look after you" I asked. I was so mad and when I saw to her needs I went home.

The next day, when I arrived, I found she had cooked me a meal; I was surprised and thought to myself, she's not as ill as she makes out.

Shortly after, her doctor saw her and told her, she was not able to live on her own any more, she had to move into sheltered accommodation, as long as the doctor said it; it was alright. He found her a place, Robert Stokes, in the Frairy and a date was set for her move, it was on a Saturday; I gathered the whole family together, hired a self drive removal van and told mum to pack all her clothes and personal belongings, and we would be there first thing in the morning.

When we arrived, she hadn't packed a single thing, so Janet and myself, set about packing what she needed; giving away things she would never use again and putting everything else in the back garden, for the bin men.

My two daughters and their husbands, arrived with the van, loaded it up and delivered it to her new address. We left her with a single bed and a kettle. My son-in-law, Steve, connected her cooker and the rest of us brought her furniture in, unpacked her clothes and put them away. We were all pretty tired, so we called it a day. The next day I went back to the new flat, scrubbed, cleaned and polished and when it was done I went back to mum and said "everything is ready all you have to do is put the key in the door, I'll come back with you."

"I'm not moving," she said "but you can't stay here all your things are in your new place, you have no cooker, no fridge, how are you going to eat"; "that's all right" she said, "the neighbours will feed me". I was so angry, tired and in need of a bath after all that cleaning, I just threw the keys at her and walked out; that was on the Sunday and I decided not to bother again.

On the following Friday my foreman Cyril, called me to his office he said there was a phone call for me; the voice on the other end of the phone asked "Is that Mrs Blake," "yes" I said, "whose calling;" It was the hospital, "do you have a mother called Iris Murray," "yes" I said. Apparently she had moved herself into her new flat on the Thursday, without telling anyone; fallen over and broken her Femur. She was in hospital for ten days and sent home in plaster. She was a nightmare until she healed and I could not afford to take time off from work, to look after her, so I was run ragged having to go there after work every day.

As the years went by, her dementia got worse and she sometimes overdosed on her medication; I had a phone call from her warden, saying she could not get my mother to answer her door and would it be alright, to let herself, in "of course" I said. She rang back a few minutes later to tell me she found mother unconscious on the floor and she was sending for the ambulance. I got to the hospital, to find mum on a trolley, in the corridor; I stayed with her, from nine o' clock in the morning, till they found her a bed at seven o'clock in the evening. When she was settled, I said "goodnight, see you tomorrow". "What are you talking about", she said, "it's only morning."

When I visited the next day she said, "I've been on that trolley for three days and they haven't given me anything to eat or drink; it was then I realised, she really had lost the plot.

Trinity House decided she needed twenty four hour day care and moved her to Steve Biddle House. She was moved in, in the February and got more and more disorientated. I will never know how she remembered my phone number but she would ring me in the middle of the night and tell me to come and get her as she didn't like it there, "if you don't I'm going to go out and get run over by a bus;" or she would say "come and make me a cup of tea, you've bought me a new kettle and I don't know how it works." "It's not a new kettle" I said; "if you want a cup of tea, pull the red cord and the nurse will come and make you one." In the end my sister told me to take the phone off the hook, so I can get some sleep.

There was worse to come; she became incontinent, which meant, I was having to scrub her carpet frequently, more washing and ironing; she would give things to people as gifts and then say it was stolen; she would hide her purse and forget where she put it, so it was a game of hunt the purse, every time I called. Then there was the business of the framed photographs on the wall; on every visit, which was four times a week, she would take me around the room and I had to explain to her who everyone in the photographs were, it became a ritual she also asked if she had any more children.

One morning, when I arrived I said, as usual "hi mum" ,she looked at me and said, "who are you" "Tricia mum". I said. "I don't know any Tricia, then after a pause, oh yes I do, you've just had a baby haven't you". No mum, I'm sixty two; she was probably mixing me up with my daughter who had recently had a daughter.

My aunty Margaret, in Canada invited my sister Janet and myself to a holiday in 1997, I said I could not go, as there was no one to look after mother; the warden said I should go because if anyone needed a holiday it was me. I asked who would be looking after mother, she said if I went to a care firm and made arrangements, as long as I paid the bill, someone would come and give her a shower and make sure she took her medication.

Well I went with an easy mind and landed in Canada the same week end that Princess Diana was killed; for some reason I was very upset and cried. The holiday was very enjoyable and we were shown all the sights. When the month was over, my aunt asked me to stay for another month "I can't I said, you wouldn't want me to neglect your sister would you;" "no my girl she said but when you get back, phone me and reverse the charges; whenever I phone your mum she says I don't know who you are, then puts the phone down and I get very upset.

I arrived back the day before her eighty fifth birthday and paid all the bills for mothers so called care; being a bit jet lagged, I decided to visit mum on her actual birthday, taking with me the cards and gifts sent by her sister, I then phoned her sister as promised and handed the phone to mum, she listened for a moment then handed the phone back to me, saying "I don't know who this woman is, you talk to her" my auntie started to cry and I had to explain it was the illness and nothing personal.

I asked my mother why she was still in her night dress and she said she had nothing else to wear; I went to the bathroom and found a mountain of dirty washing, soiled sheets and clothes. I went to take her nightdress off and found it was stuck to her body, so it was obvious she hadn't even had a shower or bath for quite a while she had an enormous ulcer on her back and was in a lot of pain. I phoned her doctor and all he said was there's nothing more I can do for your mother, this was on the twenty ninth, the day after her birthday; I had an appointment with my own doctor that afternoon and he could see that I was upset and he asked me what the problem was, so I told him I also told him that her doctor refused to see her. "Would you like me to intervene" he asked, "yes please" I said. Well my doctor phoned her doctor and he agreed to go and see her straight away, but he never did, until the following Thursday ,he took one look at her and sent for the ambulance.

My doctor said to me "you can't keep looking after your mother it is affecting your health, she needs full time care; I will give you a phone number for a care home, ring them today". When I phoned, a lady with an Irish accent answered; the first question she asked was "has she got twenty thousand pounds in the bank" "no", I said, "well in that case she will have to wait her turn like everyone else, but I will come and do an assessment tomorrow". I went to mothers the next day and waited all day for this woman to turn up, but she never did.

Any way after she was admitted to hospital she was treated for her ulcers and a few days later she developed pneumonia and went into a coma, from which she never recovered, she passed away on the thirteenth of October 1997; she was cremated a few days later.

The day after her funeral, I had a phone call from the warden of Steve Biddle; she said "your mother had a visitor today guess who it was; it was the people from the care home, they had come to do an assessment on your mother. I told them they were three weeks too late, we had her funeral yesterday". I never heard from them again.

I had no idea how much was involved in death and funerals; I had to get several copies of her death certificate, one each for the bank, funeral director, pension and insurance. Then I had to clear out her flat, get rid of her belongings and sort out her will; not that there was much left after her funeral and outstanding bills were paid. Her instructions were, whatever she had left was to be divided between her four children and of course her jewellery had to go to her favourite daughters, Janet and Geraldine. Janet refused to refused to cut short her holiday in Canada so she didn't come to the funeral; I had to ask the funeral directors to keep the ashes till my sister came home a couple of weeks later and we held another service to inter her ashes.

A brief synopsis of my children

My family consists of four children, three girls and a boy; Carol Ann married Stephen Harrison and they have two children, Sarah Ann and Matthew John. Sarah is married to Dan Wale they, have my first great grand child, Harry.

Jacqueline was married to Keith Fancett they have two daughters, Kerri and Helen. Jacqui and Keith divorced. Jacqui has since remarried to Stephen Baker and they live in New Zealand.

Patricia was married to Ernie Wattie. She had a girl and a boy, Nicola Clair and Simon Clive. She has since divorced. She and her new partner Keiron Fealy have a daughter Siannan Ciarraiann. Nicola is married to Richard Farley.

My only son, John Terence was married to Maria Chamberlain. They have a son and a daughter, Daniel John and Natasha Marie; Maria and John are divorced and Maria has since remarried.

I have loved my children one hundred and ten per cent, sometimes tough love, I'm ashamed to say, I used to take my frustrations out on them when they were small , all I wanted was for them to grow up into decent adults. I have overlooked a great many things good, bad and indifferent from them. I have been hurt by them from time to time. I don't demand they love me in return but I do demand respect; any thing less, I don't deserve. The only thing I want for them, is to be happy.

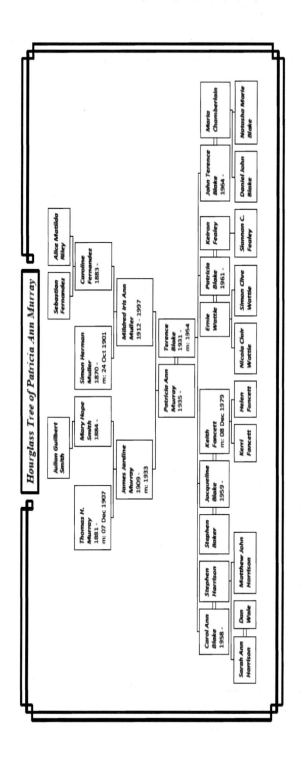

Hourglass Tree of Patricia Ann Murray

Autism Guilbert Smith

Alice Matilda Riley

Sebastian Fernandez

Caroline Fernandez 1883 -

Mary Hope Smith 1884 -

Simon Herman Muller 1870 - m: 24 Oct 1901

Mildred Iris Ann Muller 1912 - 1997

Thomas H. Murray 1881 - m: 07 Dec 1907

James Jardine Murray 1909 - m: 1933

Patricia Ann Murray 1935 -

Terence Blake 1931 - m: 1954

Maria Chamberlain

John Terence Blake 1964 -

Natasha Marie Blake

Daniel John Blake

Keiron Fealey

Sinnam C. Fealey

Patricia Blake 1961 -

Simon Clive Wattle

Ernie Wattle

Nicola Clair Wattle

Keith Fancett m: 08 Dec 1979

Helen Fancett

Kerri Fancett

Jacqueline Blake 1959 -

Stephen Baker

Carol Ann Blake 1958 -

Stephen Harrison

Matthew John Harrison

Dan Wale

Sarah Ann Harrison

Acknowledgements

My thanks to Dr Robertson for advising me to write this book, it has indeed helped me emotionally, as he predicted.

My thanks to Jane Lidiard for her invaluable help and advice, without which I would not have come this far. Also to my son John for his patience and computer skills, which are far greater than my own.

Thank you all.